Toppling the Pyramids

Toppling
the
Pyramids

REDEFINING THE WAY
COMPANIES ARE RUN

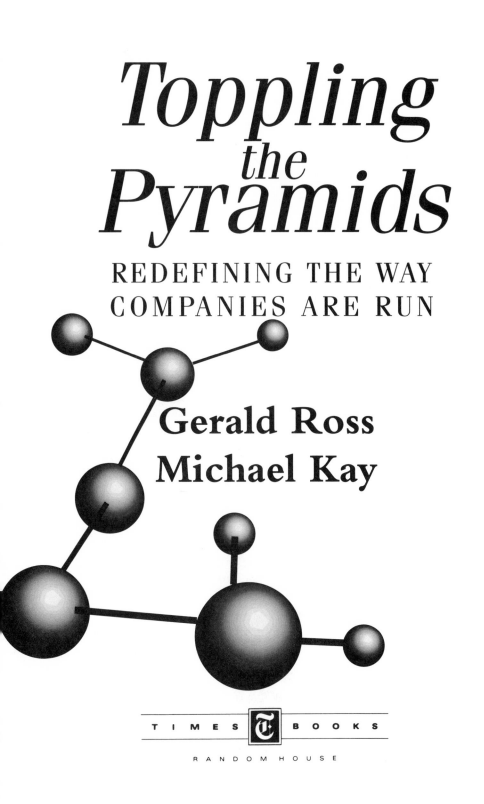

Gerald Ross
Michael Kay

TIMES 𝕿 BOOKS

RANDOM HOUSE

Library of Congress Cataloging-in-Publication Data

Ross, Gerald.
    Toppling the pyramids : redefining the way companies are
run / Gerald Ross and Michael Kay. — 1st ed.
        p.   cm.
    Includes bibliographical references and index.
    ISBN 0-8129-2341-3
    1. Industrial management—United States.   2. Organizational
change—United States.   I. Kay, Michael.   II. Title.
HD38.R596   1994
658.4'06—dc20   94-167

Manufactured in the United States of America
9   8   7   6   5   4   3   2
First Edition
DESIGN BY GLEN M. EDELSTEIN

Acknowledgments

This is the inside story of six organizations and the challenges their leaders faced as they led them through major changes. They faced the terrifying uncertainties of change, but shouldered the burden, marching on to transform their businesses. Their experiences, wrenching at the time, but fulfilling both personally and professionally, gave us insights into the emerging Molecular Organization and the stages on the way to this goal. Without them, and the other clients we worked with who do not appear in this book, nothing would have been possible. We thank them for their help and for sharing what were invigorating experiences which led without exception to competitive success.

Each of the cases describes that magic moment of revelation when the participants opened the door to their new world. We were there helping, and the stories we tell are about those moments and the events that followed—seen from our perspective. Our descriptions are accurate; however, we have not attempted to reconstruct minute details. It is sufficient for this book to know that the changes were made and made successfully. Any mistakes are, of course, our responsibility.

In three of the situations we describe—Implements, Inc.,

WCI America, and the story about Jack Kirkbride—we have changed names and identifying details such as locations and type of industry. With the other three—Ault Foods, IBM and Aetna—these are, of course, actual companies and people.

No book is written by the authors alone. We would like to thank our colleagues at Change Lab International for their help. But we would like to single out one person, Robin Davis, without whom this book would never have been either started or finished. A tower of strength, she kept us on track against the tug of a thousand other obligations as well as providing timely criticism and praise.

Consulting in change is a unique blend of helping the client find strategic insight and managing the human emotions of fear and elation. It is exhausting and consuming and puts immense pressure on the family of the change agent. Without the nurturing of our wives, Linda and Isabel, and the understanding of our children, Alexander, Philippa, Kimberley and Julia, we would never have completed the work which led to this book.

—Greenwich, 1994

Contents

Toppling the Pyramids

Introduction:
It's a New World

Opportunity comes with change. Big opportunities happen when everything is in flux. Everything is in flux now. All around us there is dislocation, stress and the breakup of established orders. Obviously, this presents a threat. Yet, for the nimble, and the fearless, it presents unparalleled opportunity.

We are living during the crucial decade of one of the half-dozen most intense periods of change the world has ever seen. The full transition to the Knowledge Age is actually happening, and most of us in management have been struggling for an operational understanding of how to capitalize on it. This book presents an organizational model—the Molecular Organization—that will allow companies, and the people who run them, to take advantage of this epic period of change. A period of change that is downright scary.

IT'S EASY TO BE OVERWHELMED BY FEAR

For tens of millions of people the end of the American Century coincides with the end of the American Dream. As we move toward the year 2000, truckers and assembly-line workers wait on unemployment lines with former chief financial officers and marketing vice presidents. Once granite-like institutions—everything from Macy's to IBM—are crumbling, taking with them an unprecedented number of chief executives. The national debt is so large that it's impossible to fathom. The United States, once the lender of last resort, is now the largest debtor the world has ever known.

Large companies watch helplessly as smaller competitors skim the most profitable portions of their markets. They can't downscale because there, too, there are new firms— often foreign ones—offering prices that they can't come close to matching. That leaves these companies in the middle, in a largely commodity business, fighting to shave fractions of a cent off the price of what they sell.

To cope, these firms react as they always have: cutting costs, firing people and shifting production offshore. This time, however, the result is not lower costs but a seeming death spiral. In 1992 alone, IBM lost $4.9 billion; General Motors lost $4 billion; Ford, $3.8 million. What is becoming clear is that we can't "downsize" our way to a new economy. We can't become healthy by deciding to be anorexic.

The ills of these companies spill over into the lives of people who work there, and indeed work everywhere. In the last ten years, per capita income has actually declined, with family earnings buoyed only because both the husband and the wife are employed. We are working harder than ever, and have more labor-saving technology at our disposal, yet we are getting poorer at a time of unparalleled opportunity. The status quo no longer works. The aristocracy of business and government is toppling. The leading companies are shunted briskly aside by others who were only recently unknown—CNN, home shopping companies and Wal-Mart. Some of the old leaders may reinvent themselves, but in the meantime, there is a bonanza of opportunity.

Technology too is exploding. We sit in living rooms munching popcorn as we watch the storming of the Russian White House. The personal computer puts intelligence at everyone's fingertips. Microchips have invaded our cars, toasters, cameras and video recorders. We are now moving into the software revolution with new ways of writing software that will allow us to mold the machine to our individual needs—whether personal or business—using its potential as an extension of our own will.

This dramatic shift in technology is rewriting the rules of how we organize ourselves and how profit can be made. The huge opportunity it is creating is because every aspect of business is touched. Such opportunity does not occur when everything is known and being improved incrementally. It happens when everything is up for grabs. The robber barons of the Victorian era did not win big just because they were ruthless. They won because they were willing to play for high stakes at a time of global expansion.

Opportunities today are easily as great. Take Bill Gates of Microsoft, rising from nowhere to become the world's youngest billionaire. All you need to know is how technology can drive fast, flexible, low-cost responses to the customers.

Throughout this book, we will see how six companies, some with their backs to the wall, have grasped opportunity from adversity: IBM, wrestling with how to focus an unwieldy global organization to better serve the customer;

Aetna Insurance, reinventing how to sell life insurance by reducing the huge overhead of an agency force; World Communications International America, riding the global information wave for instant access to the financial trading markets and news; Ault Foods, one of the largest dairies in North America, digging out profits in an industry with razor-thin margins; Implements, Inc., breaking the back of the entrenched paradigms of traditional management; and Jack Kirkbride, bringing the lonely life of a development engineer into the heady world of empowered teams.

All of these companies are on the journey to the Molecular Organization, building organizations with flexible technologies, flexible workforces and flexible economics. All of them had the felt need to change—usually due to profit pressure—but some saw the writing on the wall and started to change while they were still successful. All of them are riding the information wave.

CATCH A WAVE

Ride the wave of history. Go with the flow. As old structures break up at this point of transition, big waves are there to surf.

But you will not be able to ride any wave unless you have mastered the basics of the new world. If you want to surf, you must have balance, and for balance you need focus. Our old images of how to organize are no longer appropriate, as outmoded as the slide rule in the age of the handheld calculator.

The new Molecular Organization, which draws its imagery from biology, chemistry and the life sciences, is replacing the traditional pyramidal organization rooted in the mechanical sciences of the nineteenth century. Companies are discovering that the impossible can happen. They can dramatically lower costs by customizing to each individual customer, rather than by producing large runs of identical goods. This new technology is called Mass Customization. This technological wizardry can be coupled with highly flexible human systems that abandon the stilted lines of management command for versatile work teams that operate with little or no supervision.

Accomplishing this is not easy. It is hard to keep your balance because technology, corporate structure and organizational behavior are changing all at once. But what will come out of this chaos, when you are successful, is the creation of a flexible, low-cost organization that by being close to its customer and customizing its products to the values of the customer is a powerhouse against all competitors—domestic or foreign.

Companies making the transition to Molecular must go through different stages, each with its own challenges, bumps and traps. The six stories illustrate these issues, and from them you can learn how to take your organization into the new world.

IT'S A NEW WORLD

Markets are fragmenting. Niche competitors are swarming. Everywhere things seem increasingly complex. Yet our management systems and approaches are built for worlds of large standard markets. What we have today is a fundamental mismatch between the skills we have as managers and the skills we need.

This isn't surprising. The training of the generation in power—and worse, the generation coming to power—was in the old economics and production methods. Managers today still think in terms of multi-product companies, not multi-niche companies. They still chase market share to get often illusory economies of scale. They reflexively demand high levels of asset utilization, even when the systems required to do that slow responses and create inflexibility. These managers are suffering the ultimate irony: They are being blindsided by their own professional expertise. At a deep subliminal level they know it. They charge off in a new direction, preaching the need for "total quality," and how we must "reengineer the corporation," and no one follows. They pull levers in their organizations and nothing happens. Yet all around them are the pieces of the puzzle that will provide them with the answer to how to create a new company.

Until now, no one has put all the pieces together to form an overall image. In the absence of that image, managers have been at the mercy of all the gurus who come and go. Desperate to find answers, corporations and the people who run them have been using "silver bullets," the latest quick-fix idea that will cure them of their ills. This is the year of quality, of customer service, of empowerment. You can see it everywhere you look.

This true story is typical. George, the CEO of a major telecommunications company, is on his way to catch a plane when he stops in the airport book shop and picks up a book on Total Quality Management (TQM). About halfway through the flight, while sipping bad airline coffee, he sees the light. He now understands how to turn his struggling company around.

Once home, he plunks a copy of the book in front of every senior manager and announces, "TQM is the answer to our problems. Let's implement a total quality program. Now!" There is a flurry of activity, a general corporate call to arms. There is an explosion of activity. Teams are formed, goals set. Everyone runs around in all directions. Viewed from above it looks like a Chinese fire drill. A year later the whole program has become bogged down in minutiae and meetings. While some soldier on with missionary fervor, most who are skeptical now snipe openly at the program. The rest, who have lived through a hail of silver bullets before, simply hunker down in their offices and tell themselves this, too, shall pass.

Throughout this turmoil the same accounting, budgeting, human resource and other management processes hold that were present when the company got into trouble. Come hell, high water or the latest management fad, the way those people do things doesn't change. The result is as predictable as the sunrise. TQM becomes yesterday's flavor of the month, just like quality circles and Theory Z before that, and the boss goes running off in search of yet another idea.

This sad tale has been repeated in literally thousands of organizations over the last decade, as we sought to implement "Management by Guru." It has left us with organizations stuffed with change-resistant, cynical people who, while they may give their immediate boss the benefit of the doubt, think that their top managers are not competent to lead them.

Why is this the case? If we have had all this aggressive cost-cutting, all these reorganizations, acquisitions and divestitures, and a stream of hot new management remedies, why aren't things fixed? With dozens of university professors and consultants and bright, dedicated management—all backed up by an ocean of market surveys, powerful new improvement techniques and the latest in technology—why aren't we reaching new heights of achievement? The 1990s should have been the decade of economic boom, but all the newspaper reports say that business will be satisfied with a whimper. "Slow but steady growth is the best we can hope for" is all you hear economists and corporate executives say day after day after day.

The problem is the gurus, and the people who follow them, continue to insist on changing one thing at a time when the problem is holistic. The entire environment we operate in is changing, and you cannot work on a complex system by changing one variable and then moving on to the next. You have to work from many points at once.

Demanding more quality without changing the accounting systems measuring that quality will not work. Reengineering processes without regard to the fundamental changes needed in the underlying structure is an exercise in futility. In fairness, those who espouse silver-bullet prescriptions almost without exception point out the need for working on the whole problem. But in our experience, no client ever has. That is understandable. They have never had an overriding model with which to understand the whole system. How can you change what you cannot visualize?

This book describes the moments of revelation which started six leaders on their journey to the Molecular Organization. Some are now in their second round and making the full transition. All of them started from different places, at different levels of understanding and need. But for all of them, the changes they made were in the context of a new model, a new icon.

All of them discovered that the programs they had previously followed were not lost. When they looked under the skins of all the management fads, they saw that they were all pointing in the same direction. You cannot get a flexible low-cost, world-class, lean-production manufacturing system without empowered workers. You cannot get "quality in the eyes of the customer" without the "lean-production" techniques developed in manufacturing by the Japanese, the continuous production of a variety of multi-product assembly lines and empowered people. Empowered people are the descendants of job-enriched people, who in their growing awareness demand the tools of information systems and flexible manufacturing to do their jobs. And so it goes on until the whole experience has been had and the major characteristics of the Molecular Organization are experienced.

The leap these executives made was seeing the new world as a whole—seeing a new icon, the Molecular Organization.

The Molecular Organization is a new way of visualizing the world. It exists whole and complete as did its predecessor image—the pyramidal organization. If you visualize it, the confusion and chaos from competing but complementary programs dissipates, and the change to the new environment can be made with deliberation. But only in recent years have we known enough to conceive of the Molecular Organization in order to start building it.

The change to the new world is a process and an act of leadership will. That process starts in an odd place—with forgiveness.

BEGIN WITH FORGIVENESS

To resolve the mess that our companies find themselves in today, we must get past the self-torturing questions of "What did I do wrong? Why didn't I see this coming? How could I have stopped this from happening in the first place?" The reality is that no one could have foreseen this happening, so there is no one to blame.

We missed these changes because we were never trained to see them. From the time we were young, our parents, schools and companies taught us to think in terms of size and scope. Bigger was better. Scale will be our salvation. Only today are we discovering that although that might have been true then, it is no longer true now. Size and scale are giving way to flexibility and speed.

We are not bad people for missing this change. We are

neither incompetent nor foolish. We lived in a way of seeing the world that was right at the time but is now poisoning us and preventing us from reaching into a new life.

We came to that realization earlier than most people. Not because we are smarter, but because we have been working with many different companies, viewing the world from many different perspectives, not just one. We were inside companies and government agencies as they grappled with change. That made it possible for us to see that the fleet was being swamped, not merely individual ships. The imagery is apt. We have been living in the cusp of a rogue wave of change, a wave that we could not have foreseen. To understand that we have been ignorant is a starting point. To remain ignorant is inexcusable. CEOs will no longer be able to find solutions in a book—not even this one—and pass them on to management to implement. They will have to get down into the business and earn the right to lead, by being in the trenches of change with the employees. As the toppling heads in America's corporate boardrooms prove, leaders who are out of touch with their businesses are doomed. Now is a time for vision, but a vision that is more than operational, a vision of how we will work together in the future—the molecular way. It's the most natural way in the world.

"Molecular"—The Most Natural Organization in the World

In the early 1970s, when the State University of New York at Stony Brook held a major gala to unveil a new part of the campus, visitors thought the college had forgotten to put in sidewalks. The buildings were all up and signs were posted telling you how to get around, yet there were no paths between the buildings.

"We figured we'd wait for a year, to see where people actually walked, and then pave over those routes," we were told by the proud dean. "That just seems to make more sense than pouring concrete and watching people trample the grass because we hadn't picked the paths where people walk."

We think about that story a lot when dealing with corporations. It reminds us that every once in a while a big organization does something right. When you go back to figure out how that happened, we almost always hear the same thing.

"It was all Harry's doing," we are told. "He's the original 'thousand-pound gorilla' that gets things done come hell or high water. Harry was committed to making the project work. He got the money he needed out of the budget of some other project he was supposed to be working on. He got people to steal an hour here and two hours there to help him out, and he promised us he would take the blame if things didn't work out. We went along, dividing up the work as we went, and it worked out just great."

In other words, Harry's pirate band put the sidewalks in after the fact. Harry set the objective—creating the new project—and everything evolved from there. It's a very natural way of organizing. Indeed, it may be the only one that makes sense given today's complex, fast-moving business environment.

But Harry's approach to management—working through the informal networks to get things done—is not the way things generally operate. Sure, it is employed occasionally when someone organizes a special project or puts a task force together. But it is the exception, not the rule. Before it can become the rule, we need to change our image of the organization from the rigid pyramidal form to something infinitely more flexible.

Not everybody can be a thousand-pound gorilla like Harry, getting things done by sheer muscle. We need a structure where good, solid people can coordinate effortlessly across all the artificial boundaries and constraints of the organization.

OF ATOMS, MOLECULES, AND BUGS

The traditional management model—a pyramid with the boss on top, a couple of very senior managers beneath him, some senior managers below them, and so on down the line until you actually reach the people who do the work—is just fine if you are in a business where things don't change quickly. The pyramid structure, by definition, is slow to react because it evolved in a time when markets didn't change quickly.

Increasingly, corporations need to respond quickly. Like three-year-olds, customers want what they want when they want it. In this kind of environment, the slowness of the pyramid structure gets in the way. Within a pyramid structure, the Harrys of the world are the only way to get anything done fast.

In today's environment, what's needed is a new kind of organization, one that responds faster and is flexible. But the organization should also incorporate the lessons we learned from Harry and his group. The organization should flow with the way people really work, as the university footpaths flowed with the students' desire for the shortest route to class. It should be one where cooperation need not be forced, and where the people find the shortest route to satisfying the customer.

We call this dispersed, flexible entity the Molecular Organization. You can picture it best by imagining what the organization looks like at the atomic level. Each atom has at its center a strategic nucleus—the boss. Spinning around that nucleus are the electrons—the operating people. In this world, all the action—where the work is done—is as close to the customer as possible. Holding the whole atom together is a strong shared vision and a set of values, displacing traditional supervision.

In this world, the function of bosses is completely different. Their role is to set priorities—including financial ones —establish the company's vision and guard its culture. And that's it. According to the traditional role, bosses spend their time fighting fires—budgets blown, deadlines missed and conflicts refereed. They might get calls at three in the morning to deal with crises, or log long hours during evenings and weekends away from their family, just to keep afloat.

In the new world, the boss spends 50 percent or more of his or her time on issues with a time frame of one year and beyond, big strategic issues. Should the company introduce a new product line or move into eastern Europe? Really BIG decisions.

This new role is *more* important. The boss is freed from day-to-day operations with all their petty problems. He or she doesn't spend time putting out fires, and there are not a whole lot of meetings to call or attend. But the job is much more important because by setting priorities he or she tells the company and its employees where to spend time, energy and resources. Most of those employees expending all that effort are out in the field responding to the customer.

Both these roles are extensions of roles we are familiar with. The big change comes when we look at the "supervisors." They are no longer supervising the people who do the work—there is no need. The boss has set the agenda, so it is clear what employees are supposed to do. Once the power is pushed down to the people on the line, there really is very little to supervise. So what do the supervisors do?

Instead of being cops, checking to see where the people on the line screw up, they become a resource. They will help the frontline people learn how to make decisions. They will be more like internal consultants supporting people, rather than managers giving orders. This may take time. Many of the people who suddenly find themselves empowered will have spent their entire careers just following orders.

This simple atomic image is at the heart of understanding

the Molecular Organization. Just as atoms form to make molecules, so do operating units come together to form large organizations. They just re-create the basic structure on a larger scale. In this bigger version, the nucleus is the home office, the electrons are the operating units, but the same principles apply. The boss sits in the home office—at the center—and designs strategy and is concerned with the future of the whole system. Operating units are focused on their markets and their customers. Middle management—what little there is of it—provides the linkages between the two, helping to manage the vision and values.

But, you will ask, isn't this exactly what happens in the pyramidal organization? What's different? The difference lies in the structure's ability to deal with and adapt to complexity. As we shall see, the molecular form is simply more efficient.

But why can't the old form be made to work faster? Why do we need a new form? To understand that, we need to make a short digression to a distant relative of us all—the amoeba.

A SIMPLE ORGANISM

The amoeba is a very simple organism. All it does is eat, excrete and divide to form other amoebas. All this is fine. The problem starts when amoebas divide and find themselves in large clusters. When that happens, life for the amoeba on the inside of the cluster becomes most unpleasant. Being cut off from the outside, the innermost amoeba finds itself eating what others have excreted.

To escape this situation, amoebas need some form of organization that will create channels to bring fresh water to the amoebas on the inside and take away their wastes.

But this in turn creates a problem, a hydraulic one. The

amoebas can't have water flowing in at the same time that waste is flowing out. (You can't suck and blow at the same time.) They need valves. And if you have valves, you need a way to control them, which in turn gives rise to a nervous system and primitive brain.

Flash forward a bit. After millions of years our amoeba has become a bug. It has legs whose only jobs are to help it walk and stand. It also has wings, to help it fly, and a brain, whose job it is to watch out for birds and to plan the next migration. The bug is both more specialized and decentralized in its functions than the amoeba, and at the same time it is more centralized because the brain is making decisions that affect the whole body.

Life for the amoeba was pretty simple. It sat in a simple environment and responded to it. By the time it becomes a bug, it has a much more complex life. The bug has to answer a whole host of questions: where to live; who to mate with; whether to migrate; and so on. It has to process much more —and different—kinds of information. As it goes through the various stages of increasing complexity, its changing structure must keep pace with the level of information it has to process. Its eyes gather complex visual information. Its antennae sense other aspects of its environment. Its wings pick up the airflows over the their surfaces. This is a long way from the simple one cell amoeba.

That is exactly what is happening in the shift from pyramidal to Molecular Organizations. The bug and the Molecular Organization are structures designed to deal with more complexity than their predecessors. Whereas the bug has to worry about predators, the Molecular Organization has to worry about changing markets, global competition, more technical options and so on. The organization evolves to adapt to its changing environment.

Like the bug, which continually senses its environment and reacts to or anticipates events at great speed, the Molecular Organization has its nerves very close to the surface, continually sensing the changes in the customer base and making adjustments to its offerings. It has multiple interfaces with the customer, not just a single one limited to the sales force. Product development and other functions now interact frequently with the customer, sensing new emerging needs.

The molecular image captures the ability of an organization to expand or contract more easily—by adding or shedding atoms or molecules—without destroying the whole system. For example, many of the functions that used to be in the old head offices are now much more self-contained and are either in the field or completely outsourced to third parties. As we will see through this book, the molecular image is simply more flexible.

CENTRALIZE OR DECENTRALIZE? YES!

This shift to the molecular also eliminates one of the conundrums of modern business: whether to centralize or to decentralize.

Over the last twenty years, exploding technology, burgeoning markets and globalization have made the environment increasingly complex. In response, organizations have gone through continual cycles of centralization and decentralization as they tried to find some way to make the old, outmoded pyramidal model work a bit better. One year staff groups are herded into the head office to focus their resources. The next, they are banished out to the extremities of the organization to cut down on overhead. The result has been constant turmoil.

But does an organization operate most efficiently when it's centralized or decentralized? To find out, let's again use biology as our model, and try to create a biological equivalent of a minor business crisis: a paper cut.

Think about what happens when you cut your finger opening a letter. The brain assesses the problem. It signals the antibodies to deal with an invasion of germs. Then the brain leaves the job of repair to the affected cells. To bring the example full circle, we can say that the brain has pushed the responsibility for repair on down the line.

The parallel to our molecular model of organization holds perfectly. The cells (the people on the line) have all the skills they need to deal with local phenomena. The organs and immune systems (our middle managers) deal with those issues affecting multiple local sites, while the brain (the boss) oversees the whole system and worries about issues affecting the whole body.

Under the old pyramid model, the brain would have attempted to solve every problem the cell encountered, and as a result would have become hopelessly overloaded. Anyone who has been in an overcentralized organization can appreciate that fact.

In real life, the pyramid's centralist bias tends to overload the brain, a fact not immediately apparent because minor crises pile up and the urgent drives out the important. Eventually everything grinds to a halt. The top of the business then tries to solve the problem of paper cuts by developing a permanent, specialized operation dedicated to paper cuts. It builds in costs and procedures and slows itself down.

Far better is what the human body does. It decentralizes repair functions (clotting and skin repair) while coordinating the whole process of healing. As we shall see, this is exactly how the Molecular Organization functions. It takes a set of skilled people and groups them swiftly around a problem—continuously and automatically.

Much as Harry pulled together the people and resources he needed across the organization to address a specific issue, the Molecular Organization continually forms and re-forms groups as needed, rather than adhering to the rigid reporting lines and management structures of the bureaucracy.

With the organization focused around the customer, the various departments—sales, production, etc.—are able to work together toward the same goal: responding to the customer's needs. This teamwork allows fast response time and faster product development. But in the molecular organization, this teamwork goes far beyond "cross-functional" cooperation to build working networks or "communities"—like Harry did—to serve the customer.

How do you get to this nirvana? Well, you start with understanding that the Molecular Organization is inevitable. The molecular revolution is jointly fed by both our desire for a "designer lifestyle" to express our individuality and our technical ability to deliver it.

LET'S GO SHOPPING

The Stamford Mall is in suburban Connecticut, but it could be anywhere. Contained within its four floors is a microcosm of the consuming world as it has developed over the last thirty years. Anchoring the mall are branches of three major department stores: Saks, Macy's and J.C. Penney. There must be over a hundred boutique chains represented. Williams-Sonoma sells a kitchen experience. Kay-Bee Toys and F.A.O. Schwarz tap into our children's hunger for the new, the novel and our guilt to provide it. Foot Locker, and its rivals such as The Athlete's Foot, sell every kind of sneaker imaginable.

Enter the food court and look at the soft drinks. In the old days it was simple. There were just five choices: Coke, Pepsi, orange, 7 Up and root beer. Today, there are a dozen kinds of Coke alone: Coke, Coca-Cola Classic, diet Coke,

Caffeine Free Coca-Cola Classic, Caffeine Free diet Coke, cherry Coke, diet cherry Coke and so on. And let's not forget about raspberry-flavored seltzer water, Orangina and the fruit juices and sports drinks that are available.

Enter one of the gourmet food stores and try to buy a pound of coffee. Regular or decaf? Sure, that kind of choice is to be expected. But if you decide on regular you still have to pick from Jamaican Blue, Kona, mocha chocolate and fifty others. And each regular coffee has a decaffeinated equivalent. Even then you aren't done. What grain size do you want? What roast? Let's try a simpler decision: buying a phone.

"Yes, sir. Would you like Euro-phones, antique phones, futuristic phones, portable phones, fax phones, cellular phones, waterproof phones?"

"Well, actually I was looking for the old, common black phone, the kind mother used to have. The one with the heavy weight and solid feel."

"Ah, yes. The 'nostalgia niche.' "

What we see in the mall is an example of designer lifestyles. It is hard when you walk around a shopping mall that has more than a hundred different clothing stores to remember when this kind of choice was unavailable. Indeed, if you are under thirty-five, you can't remember. This kind of variety has been available your entire life. The only way you know that lack of choice used to be standard is through history books.

A customer could have his Model T in any color he wanted as long as it was black, Henry Ford said in the first part of this century, and things didn't change much in the decades that followed. Imported goods of just about any kind were rare. That was true not only in the United States, but around the world. In the 1960s, imports made up only 5 percent of the U.S. gross domestic product. People thought they were getting variety because they could buy a few imported goods, but that really wasn't the case.

So how did all this variety start? As an unintended consequence of mass production's very success. In order to drive down the costs of the factories created in the post–World War II era, new markets had to be found abroad to absorb the ever-increasing production runs. At first manufacturers in Europe turned to exports as a fundamental strategy for gaining the volume and economies of scale enjoyed in America. They had to export to remain competitive. In companies such as Volvo, for example, executives might say: We can't stay in business by selling cars just in Sweden. We need to sell them in the rest of Europe and North America as well.

As a result, we consumers were flooded with all kinds of goods from all over the world. We drank French wine, ate Danish butter and drove Italian cars. For the first time, we experienced choice. But this was because of expanding world trade, not because the manufacturers were really producing variety. A Volvo was a Volvo was a Volvo, a basic, boxy-looking form of transportation.

Still, we were confronted with a cornucopia of options. All of a sudden we could buy a Renault, a Fiat, a Jaguar or a Plymouth. We acquired a taste for French wine, Danish butter, German beer and Japanese television sets. Our parents dined on meat and potatoes, buying fruits and green vegetables only when they were briefly available in season. We have fettuccine Alfredo and California oranges, raspberries and arugula year round. We became hooked on choice. And so a major change in the marketplace had begun.

But once the genie is out of the bottle, it is hard to put it back in. Once exposed to choice, we wanted more. This was what the 1970s were all about. We started to say things like: I want my Volvo with air-conditioning because I have a place in Florida. Or we said we wanted it with four-wheel drive because of our ski house in the mountains.

"And as long as you're at it, would you add a couple of pinstripes, a fancier set of wheel covers, and . . ."

In the 1980s, choice went ballistic. New niche products emerged in all parts of our economy—designer beers, joggers' Walkmen, exotic safari travel, junk bonds, children's books with your own taking part in the story. On the plane the other day, we asked for the airline's list of special meals. There were twenty-four specialized cuisines, not just individual meals. We had a choice of Muslim, macrobiotic, low-fat, kosher, lactose-free, salt-free and on and on and on.

Twenty years ago, these specialized niches would have been considered as idiosyncratic fringe markets, rather than serious considerations for a mass marketer. Now, however, the mass markets themselves are disappearing, fragmented into tiny specialized niches. This erosion and the ultimate disappearance of mass markets has undermined the very economies of virtually all major businesses. How would Henry Ford react to a customer's demand for a midnight-blue four-wheel-drive car with a CD player in the trunk? He would probably reiterate the features available on his standard Model T, or today's modern equivalent. And he would lose the sale to someone else who could deliver exactly what the customer, you and me, wants.

People like to express their individuality. Look around at the shoppers in the Stamford Mall. They are all dressed differently. They're wearing different jewelry, have different hair styles, makeup, shoes, belts and accessories. Each person is making an individual statement. Each is saying: *I'm here!*

If we were to return with them to their homes, we would find the individuality extends to all their possessions: stoves, refrigerators, stereos, television sets, carpets, beds, knives, forks and spoons. Everything selected to create the designer lifestyle.

The impact of this burgeoning variety on business has been profound. In the new world of small niches, everyone is a niche player. The only question is how many niches you cover. If you are a multi-niche player, you need to be able to deliver variety at low cost, or the specialized player will win.

This fragmentation of markets is at the very root of the Molecular Organization and half the reason for its inevitability. Mass production technology was aimed at the production of standardized products for large standardized markets. As variety entered the scene, the economies of scale at the base of mass production broke down. The other half of this story is our technical response. Exploiting the potential of information technology, we were able to adjust our production systems to serve that variety. Enter mass customization.

MASS CUSTOMIZATION: THE ENGINEERS MEET MARKETING

Consider the problem of mass production. Ever since Adam Smith described it, and Eli Whitney—a gunsmith who invented manufacturing with standard interchangeable parts—made it real in the late eighteenth century, manufacturing has followed a simple set of rules: Standardize the product; break it into components; create specialized operations to make those components (usually on dedicated equipment); then go for volume.

This whole logic is being overturned by fragmenting markets. You can no longer try to capture a mass market with a standard product. There is always another competitor providing something the customer wants more exactly. If you insist on going after the mass market anyway, the only way you can get the buyer to give up customization is to offer him a lower price. Do that often enough and you are in a commodity business, with low margins and little money to reinvest. Indeed, much of American industry is now on a trip to extinction.

By this point the production line has become so automated, and its equipment so specific to particular products, that our factories have become more and more inflexible. The development of this inflexibility was demonstrated by William Abernathy in his study of the auto industry in which he traced an extinction scenario for the car industry rooted in assumptions it has accepted since the early part of this century.

In 1903, Buick moved the engine from the middle of the car, under the seat, to the front, where the horse used to be, and where his competitors had begun placing it, in order to provide easy access. The transition was not difficult. The folks in the shop jimmied around with the chain drives, and after a few false starts got the whole thing up and running. Most cars have had their engines in the front ever since.

Contrast this scenario to the 1960s, when Volkswagen went from rear to front engine drive. It cost the company hundreds of millions of dollars and nearly put VW out of business. Similarly, in the 1970s and 1980s, the U.S. automobile industry went into convulsions—and near bankruptcy—trying to shift from rear- to front-wheel drive. The cost of adapting to a changing environment had increased dramatically as we automated production to achieve economies of scale.

In the early days of the automobile industry—just as in the personal computer industry today—innovation happened rapidly. New features such as electric lights, four-wheel brakes, the enclosed cab, heaters, and easier-to-shift engines appeared from one year to the next. The result was that people rushed out to buy the new products because of the new features. For the industry, this meant that substantial additional revenue was generated with relatively minor additional cost.

Innovation, however, peaked in the mid-1920s, and the focus started to shift to production economies that could be obtained through increasing scale. By 1940, the basic American car had been invented. It had a V-8 engine, automatic transmission and power steering. From this point on, while there were occasional technological improvements, competition was overwhelmingly based on cost. This, in turn, encouraged further automation, which allowed the automobile companies to produce their cars even cheaper. That raised the battle on price another notch, which in turn spurred the need for lower costs to remain competitive, and so it went year after year.

Fast-forward to the 1970s. In response to the energy crisis, Ford went into a mammoth development effort to produce the firm's first small car—the Escort. By this time, so much new tooling was required, involving the creation of whole new factories, that the cost of introducing the new model skyrocketed. For the first time in automotive history, the cost of developing a new car exceeded the profit that the new model could ever earn.

This is an extinction scenario, much like a population of squirrels multiplying in the face of a rapidly disappearing food supply. It doesn't take long to figure what will happen to the squirrels. The good news was that the Escort became the world's best-selling car—a recipe for fat dividends in the old days. The bad news was that Ford lost money on every Escort it produced. Having a bestseller and losing money at the same time had never happened before.

Information systems changed all this. In the 1970s and 1980s, computer-controlled tools and manufacturing systems started to emerge. By the mid-1980s the continuous production of variety was normal. The impossible had been achieved in the factory.

Today, that productive potential is being exploited by marketers. Instead of merely responding to market demand, it is being used to drive demand by adding to the variety in the market. Customized goods that can be produced quickly is the name of the game today. And, as the engineers become ever more efficient, we are moving to true "batch of one," where individual products are made for specific individuals at prices less than those of mass production.

It sounds wonderful, but this incredible technical feat has created a major problem for management that can only be solved by seeking a new form of organization with the managerial flexibility to match fragmented demand with highly specified products and services. The old managerial approaches of mass production were a fundamental mismatch with the potential of the production systems.

CORPORATE INDIGESTION

Why is exploding variety such a problem for companies? Why can't they simply respond to the new demands from their customers? The problem is that when Henry Ford standardized the shop floor, he also standardized all management decision-making processes. He created a standardized procurement process, standardized accounting and budgeting, standardized compensation and the like. The production example was too powerful to resist. From this standardization emerged the overall principle called "management by exception." In this approach everything was to be handled by preset standard procedures, and only when there was a discrepancy, such as a variance from budget, would management's attention be required. Management would then bring things back under control—i.e., within standard tolerances.

Today, if you walk into almost any business of any size, you will find thick manuals that outline standard product development, manufacturing, accounting and other processes and procedures. In this traditional world, exceptions are anathema to the system. Any kind of variation requires special attention and therefore additional cost. This is intolerable, so companies try to avoid serving special needs.

Thus, they turn up their noses at emerging niche opportunities as being too small, not economic. Ask a major brewer such as Anheuser-Busch, for example, to make ten thousand gallons of a designer beer, and you are likely to be told they can't even think of handling an order unless it involves 10 million gallons. If Marie Antoinette were alive today, she might say, "Let them drink Bud." However, because you and I still demand our mug of Australian-style lager, small, agile breweries come in and skim the foam—the small-volume, high-margin opportunities—off the top of the market. This leaves the large traditional firms to battle in areas that are doomed to become commodities.

Confronted with this new situation, many industries began shipping production overseas, closing plants and launching endless head-count reductions—none of which seems to make the problems go away. In fact, the problems often get worse.

Look what has happened in the personal computer business. The mighty IBM is locked in a never-ending battle with cheap clones and is desperately trying to find a way out. The battle has already cost more than 150,000 IBM employees their jobs. But that is not unusual. Once a company finds itself locked into a commodity business, the usual result is frequently a death spiral of ever more frequent cost-cutting, accompanied by downsizing and shipping production offshore. All this goes to prove that a company cannot find its way to corporate health by starving itself to death.

The fundamental management problem is to move—in the face of fragmenting markets and computer-driven mass customization of products—from "management by exception" to "management of exception." Enter the flat, dispersed Molecular Organization.

The Molecular Organization is then the child of two forces that have interacted with each other to create a dramatically more complex world. Rising fragmentation of the market kicked off by a competitive search for the volumes to sustain the economies of scale at the root of mass production had been fed by a technical ability to produce variety. Variety begat the demand for more variety. This in turn stimulated greater technical innovation until the techniques of mass customization coalesced everything into a new approach to production.

This technical capability was now sitting under a management system focused in entirely the opposite direction—toward the elimination of variety. The strains of that seismic fault line have resulted in the turmoil in management science that we have felt for the last twenty years.

Flexible management was inevitable, but until now no one has pulled together a comprehensive picture of this new world. No one has answered the question: What is it like to live in a molecular world?

LIVING MOLECULAR

Just as Henry Ford transferred the logic of mass production to standardized management, we are finding a transfer of logic from mass customization to flexible management today. The reason is simple. Productive technologies, and the management systems used to exploit them, are tightly linked.

In mass production, executives manage standardization— standard products and services for large, mass markets. In the molecular world of mass customization, executives are seeking to define and create custom products for individuals. In the factory, that means creating modular products and then putting them together in an infinite range of options. This is similar to the way personal computers are put together by

Dell—boards, chips, modems, screens and so on are combined in a distinctive package for each individual customer.

In management, it means a fundamental mindset change from being product-oriented to being market- and customer-oriented. In the mass production world we thought in terms of companies as portfolios of products and services. In the new world we think in terms of niches, with big players being multi-niche. But managers and consultants have been talking about the need to be customer-driven and market-driven for at least ten years.

What's new in the Molecular Organization is a molding of all business operations to fit the customer. Anything that does not add value to that customer is eliminated or adjusted. You must do that. If you don't, someone else will. This requires a tremendous knowledge of the customer and mechanisms for bringing that new knowledge into the business. No longer can you drive the business from commonly available statistics. All your competitors can do that. Today you need specific insight into what the customer values, insight into the customer's strategic, and in some cases psychic, needs.

This focus on the customer demands a tight, agreed-upon definition of who the customer is. You can no longer talk about "consumers" or "intermediaries." Today you must specify which subset of customers you are targeting and talk specifically about what gives you a competitive advantage over your competitor in going after that group.

Discovering that focus is the common starting point in all our cases. Without it, there is no vision. Asking the simple question "Who is the customer and what does he or she value?" is the most fertile approach to changing any organization.

Products that the customer designs or actions the customer can initiate at his or her whim are areas to explore. In this world, empowerment of the operating people and the customer is not an option—it is the only way you can get the flexibility you require. The pyramidal structure will not allow you to act fast enough.

Empowerment is important not only because it provides flexibility, but also because it helps reduce costs. Pushing decision-making ability out to the people who actually deal with the customer is the only way you can eliminate the management overhead that kills many large corporations.

Indeed, in the Molecular Organization, the whole way of thinking about operational cost structure changes. In the mass production world, most thinking was cost-plus. Often whole industries acted unconsciously to sustain accepted cost practices. That thinking put companies in a vise. They were trapped between the price the market was willing to pay and the price they had to charge to generate adequate shareholder return.

Niche players broke the back of cost-plus thinking, just as their fast product reactions changed development. Speed and flexibility in product development are central.

But how fast is fast? "Fast" means being able to introduce new products or services faster than your competitors can copy them! And how do you get the organization committed to develop products quickly? In the traditional organization, the time spent in a product development cycle just to get the go-ahead to make a new product can be substantial. In some cases we have seen, it is the longest single period involved.

In the molecular world, the decision to proceed can be made far faster because there is already common agreement on strategy based on what the customer needs—the market pervades the business. In the old world, having parts of the businesses insulated from the market was commonplace.

But even when every component of the business has its own economic base, the game is not over. Even though an individual factory may be efficient on its own, the costs of shared facilities and overall management coordination can make it uncompetitive. The customer is not willing to pay extra to maintain a fancy head office, baroque administrative systems and the other costs of management integration.

How low do these costs have to go? The bar that a multi-niche company has to get under is the management costs set by the efficient niche competitors who are not carrying those costs of management. There can be no other marker. Neither cost reductions nor operational flexibility can be achieved without very different behavior.

Command and control is dead. Empowerment is one manifestation of a wider behavioral approach that includes self-management and the automatic regulation of costs. In a world of little middle management, self-regulation of action, costs and accountability is the only way to stop the business from going bankrupt. In this world, not only are people responsible for their actions through their membership on a team, but they may have to carry the costs of serving the customer directly to ensure effective control of those costs.

Few organizations have taken the integrated approach we have been talking about. Many organizations today have adopted one or more of the characteristics of the new Molecular Organization, like cross-functional teamwork. However, few have put together the total picture, including the accounting, financial, human resource and other dimensions of the organization.

A holistic approach cannot be achieved without a complete image, a simple model for people to work with. The Molecular Organization is that image.

Patterns of Change —Order out of Chaos

Over the last decade, we have been exposed to every conceivable kind of organization from global corporate behemoths, major charitable organizations and large government bureaucracies to small operations. Some were just putting a toe in the water, initiating change for the first time. Others have seen wave after wave of turmoil as their leadership has tried to make their organizations more competitive.

On the surface, these organizations had very different kinds of challenges. Some were facing the possibility of being completely closed down or sold. Some got religion from total quality management or perhaps reengineering and were trying to reinvent the way they worked. Others had experienced a change of leadership at the top and the new person wanted to put his or her unique stamp on the organization. The organizations had anywhere from hundreds to hundreds of thousands of employees.

These varied experiences had a common thread: All had lost touch with their customer. And their customer was changing faster then they were! These companies simply couldn't keep up with their customer. They couldn't easily adapt to each customer's special needs, and they couldn't keep up with their competitors, who were often smaller, more agile and glued to the marketplace. These companies tripped over each other's functional and departmental barriers. The marketing people wouldn't talk to product development, so the products were far off the mark from what the customer needed. Product development wouldn't talk to the marketing people, so they didn't properly support many of the products that already existed, nor did they provide any really useful information on customer needs.

All of the organizations were struggling to *understand the customer.* In working with them, we realized that all these organizations were trying to reinvent themselves, to produce hot new products quickly, to provide excellent service and to create flexible administrative systems. In short, companies want to delight their customers—to win and hold their loyalty.

Over the years, we have noticed that there are levels of sophistication across these organizations in understanding the customer. At the basic level, some companies are just beginning to "think customer," particularly in parts of the company that normally have little to do with customers. Traditionally people in, say, the legal department or even in manufacturing argue: "We don't have to worry about the customer. We pay marketing a lot of money to do that. That's not our job!" Most people never think that they ought to concentrate on the customer.

One day we were running a workshop with a major

client and arrived early so that we could get some photo-copying done in the hotel. We went down to the concierge, who promised the copies in half an hour. At the appointed time, we went down to collect the copies and returned to the meeting room to distribute them to the participants. To our horror, we discovered that the top five pages were miss-ing!

We returned to the concierge to find out what had hap-pened to the remainder. He threw up his hands: "I didn't copy them. It was done in the back office." Incredulous at his lack of concern, we said, "Wait a minute, we are *your* customer and we don't care whether you are the janitor, the receptionist or the manager. You represent the hotel." "Not I," he replied. "I work for an outside contractor. I'm not on the hotel staff." He did what many employees do, blamed someone else for not delivering—"It's not my fault!"

In contrast, some organizations have shrink-wrapped themselves around the customer, with all the major functions such as accounting, manufacturing and human resources fo-cused on their role in adding value to the customer. In such environments, the plant is capable of customizing each indi-vidual order to the specific customer. For example, Stew Leonard's, the noted supermarket, offers the customer a fla-vor blender to permit him or her to blend the flavors in each yogurt container to suit his or her own individual taste.

We have identified five levels of understanding the cus-tomer:

- **Stage 1—The product-focused organization.** Most traditional companies are at this level. They maximize the size of their productive capacities by addressing large-scale mass markets. The fortunes of General Motors, Campbell Soup and Westinghouse were built on this foundation. In this world, "bigger is always better," because it brings more financial and marketplace muscle.

The overriding driving force is to "fill the plants," filling idle capacity at almost any cost. Thus the airlines will go to almost any lengths to avoid flying "empty seats." A computer company with an underused plant started to build electrical parts having nothing to do with the product, just to cover the staggering overhead.

When the going gets tough, organizations at this level have little choice but to let people go and to close down facilities. Since most costs are fixed, whole pieces of the operation have to be discarded. The sacred mantra of the bottom line is used as a threat to people's jobs and security.

There is little flexibility. General Motors, for example, had to close dozens of plants and have some sitting idle while others employed a full three shifts and could barely handle the work. The plants were too specialized to be adaptable. Companies like this have become "prisoners of scale."

The organizations at this stage typically have tried numerous programs in quality or similar areas, all of which have made marginal improvements, but none of which have fundamentally changed the business. Worse, the constant barrage of new programs has often left the employees cynical or skeptical. The leadership challenge is to make people believe in the idea of changing and to provide employees with a sense of confidence and destination.

• **Stage 2—The "customer-driven" culture.** A rude awakening awaits many people who are deep inside the organization; they have to all "think customer." Even those who develop the actual products often see themselves as technical wizards who "know better" than the customer. It is like pulling teeth to get an organization that for years has been focused on internal bureaucracy and politics to look outward at the real world of the marketplace.

Years ago, the railroads made the mistake of saying that they were in the railroad business, rather than in the transportation business, and completely lost out to the burgeoning trucking and airline businesses. Most people see themselves in the context of the product or service they provide. "I'm in the auto parts business," or "the insurance business." They find it completely foreign to say: "I'm in the personal financial security business," for example. As a result, we see daily examples in the newspapers of prestigious companies who have "lost their customer" because they defined their business in an outdated way. Thus learning to look at the business from the outside in, from the customer's perspective, is itself a major triumph.

The management challenge at this stage is to break down the barriers between the different functions, such as between marketing and product development, and to build teamwork and cooperation within the organization. Working together builds a shared sense of the business as a whole, rather than as one of individual fiefdoms. At this point people often resist change and start backsliding into the old turf wars.

• **Stage 3—The market-segment-driven business.** A tight focus on a specific set of customers is the key to this stage. Ralph Lauren, for example, is a business totally focused on the "nostalgia niche"—the world of sepia photographs, picnic baskets and leather luggage—the "good old days." In contrast, the typical department store often presents a smorgasbord of general merchandise, with little focus in the market.

At this level, the driving force is not "being big for the sake of being big," like Sears, but to be the most highly profitable in carefully selected parts of the market. This is not McDonald's, but Starbucks Coffees. Starbucks prides itself on pandering to our discriminating taste buds with ever more exotic coffees that, only a few months ago, we never knew existed. This is the world of Ben & Jerry's, who tracks our fickle fantasies like a shark.

The key to achieving this is lightning-quick flexibility in the production and distribution of the product or service.

General Electric, for example, has moved from production schedules for appliances measured in months to a five-day delivery, custom-tailored to the exact mix of models purchased in an individual store. This mass customization has virtually eliminated large inventories of unsold models plus all the intermediary warehousing, handling and accounting.

Companies at this stage typically launch into major "reengineering" efforts, painfully mapping out all the critical processes in their business, from product development to production to distribution. In so doing, they find thousands of tiny things that can be improved—wasted steps, lags and inefficiencies. This process can result in what some have called a "culture of continuous improvement."

The trap at this stage is that companies simply reengineer the old way of doing things rather than reinvent the new. Product development, for example, often proceeds in a linear sequence of activities, rather like a relay race, where each player passes the baton to the next one. Everything is fine until one player stubs his or her toe. Then the whole team comes down because everything is so tightly linked. Reengineering these kinds of processes may provide some improvement but will simply reinforce the traditional way of doing things.

Alternatively, product development can be looked at more as a soccer game with all the players concurrently on the field. The process is not sequential but interactive. Everybody knows that the goal is at the end of the field and that the game lasts ninety minutes. However, nobody knows where the ball will be in five minutes. The use of cross-functional product development teams reflects this new paradigm, with marketing, human resources, manufacturing and others all involved together.

• **Stage 4—The market-centered organization.** At this point, the organization starts to form itself around a specific opportunity in the market, bringing together all the relevant parties that need to be coordinated to serve the customer. This means bringing in not only the obvious people, like those from manufacturing, marketing and product development, but also those in the key support functions, like finance, human resources and procurement. All of these parties need to operate seamlessly in the interests of the customer. These people form a "community of common interest"—a group that is mutually interdependent.

We use the word "community" because, in our personal lives, we all belong to a variety of communities simultaneously. We belong to a church, a family, a department in the company, a Girl Scout group and a local charity. We are part of all of these at the same time. We are not "owned" by any one, but have important responsibilities in each. Periodically, we may have to reassess these commitments and realign ourselves accordingly.

Most organizations are not organized around markets. They are organized around products. A few months ago, we switched banks because our original bank looked at us from a product perspective. We would call up and the conversation would go something like this: "Hello, who would you like to talk to?" they would say. Our reply was "The bank!" "No, no," they would reply, "do you want to speak to the personal checking, the mortgage, the commercial departments?" "Yes," we said. "All of the above." The bank had sliced us up conveniently into its products. But we wanted to transact business across the internal boundaries.

The challenge here is to learn how to work together across the grain of the organization—the various departmental and functional boundaries. This is a question not just of teamwork, but of the reinvention of budgeting, decision-making, resource allocation and other key processes to focus on a particular market.

It requires completely reinventing all the management decision-making processes to wrap around the customer. For example, how does the bank service you and me when we may have checking accounts, a personal loan, a mortgage, a small business and a retirement savings plan? How do they present one unified face to us? How do they rethink their information systems so that they know, for example, how much money they make on us across all the products and services?

With the market-centered organization, the participants hang their hats in various parts of the organization, but come together to capitalize on a common opportunity. These communities are in effect the embryonic form of the new Molecular Organization.

• **Stage 5—The new Molecular Organization.** Here the organization formally reorganizes itself, including the budgeting, human resource and other management processes, around high priority markets. The organization that results is not merely a flattened pyramid or even an upside-down pyramid. It looks like a "molecule" because the market is at the center. Everything is designed to focus on it.

At this point, the flexible technology comes together with the highly responsive cross-boundary management processes to create an entirely new kind of enterprise as different from the traditional Industrial Age enterprise as the latter was from the cottage industry in the eighteenth century.

The challenge here is to take advantage of the extraordinary nimbleness of the business to exploit very high-margin niche markets where others fear to tread. In Japan, for example, Nissan has introduced very small volume "nostalgia-mobiles" in the 1950s tradition, where the total model run is about 10,000 units over the life of the model. In Detroit, the figure would be more like 500,000, and then it would be on a per annum basis.

The opportunity here is to enjoy all the advantages of scale while having the responsiveness of a small, scrappy

niche player. It is like having your cake and eating it too—
the best of both worlds!

The potential trap here is that, in pushing operational
decision-making down, management neglects its true function, developing an effective organization-wide strategy, including moving into new products and market areas.

Each of these stages represents a progression in the organization's understanding and responsiveness to the customer.
While the stages are sequential, however, companies can
omit certain stages; for example, a traditional Stage 1 company can move directly to a Stage 4 market-centered organization situation, but the effort required is more monumental.

Throughout this book, we are going to examine companies at each stage of this evolution to learn more about the
challenges and successes they encountered. We will tell the
stories of those making this transition. Each illustrates some
of the major issues and challenges involved at a specific stage
as follows:

Implements, Inc., is the story of a very traditional company
trying to get change off the ground at *Stage 1.*

WCI America demonstrates the transition to *Stage 2,* building
a customer-driven culture throughout all parts of its organization and dealing successfully with the early resistance based
on cynicism and skepticism.

Jack Kirkbride represents another *Stage 2* situation, seen from
the perspective of a corporate guerrilla, taking on the accumulated overburden of a very traditional culture.

Ault Foods, a Sealtest and Häagen Dazs dairy, was catapulted
into *Stage 3,* out of the miseries of a purely cost-driven business by its discovery of the economic magic of mass customization technology.

IBM originated a novel way of seamlessly serving the customer across geographical, functional and product boundaries by using the market-centered organization of *Stage 4*.

Aetna pioneered an advanced form of the Molecular Organization by leaping directly to *Stage 5*.

Leaving Home

Implements, Inc., is an extreme example of a company starting the journey from the pyramidal to the Molecular world. Insular, traditional and bureaucratic, it had developed a strong culture totally inappropriate for the modern world. It vividly displayed most of the ills of the inwardly focused, mass-production environment.

The leader was faced with a classic dilemma: how to get his management team to rally around him and how to get them to start the change. Not only were they not in financial trouble, they had been under no dramatic pressure from the parent. But, Larry Willatt had a vision of the new world and he wanted to see it implemented. The question was how.

Implementing a new vision is easier if it falls conveniently under an accepted label like "Quality." But if there isn't one handy—and in this case there was not —you cannot manufacture one. You have to change the environment of the discussion first so that management has bought in to a completely different idea of how to manage.

This kind of process is tough to manage, and especially tough for a team-oriented leader such as Larry. But as we will see, it can be done.

Larry moved his team out of Stage 1. He resolved the basic problem of getting buy-in and commitment from his top team while resolving the other major issue of Stage 1, the downsizing of the organization.

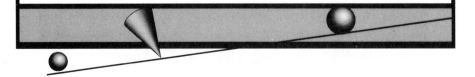

The conversation had started, as airline conversations do, with a short, meaningless complaint about the service. That broke the ice, and Larry Willatt told us he was flying to New York to meet with executives of the conglomerate that owned the company to talk about its sale.

There was no doubt that the division was being sold to provide the parent with capital, and Larry told us he could see a miserable year ahead as the carcass was picked over by interested parties looking for a deal.

"And we were making such incredible progress," Larry said. "We were really beginning to get our minds around a new way of doing business. Pushing stuff down the organization, getting all of our people out in the field more involved. We were really beginning to barrel along."

Well, everyone is entitled to exaggerate when talking to a stranger, particularly one you've just discovered is a consultant.

"The problem we're having is with the culture," Larry added a little later on in the flight. "Do you know our part of the manufacturing business?" Another point of contact. We had mutual friends, and Larry knew some of the clients we had worked with in this insular segment of manufacturing. "Then you understand how it is."

We did. Larry's company operated in an intensely conservative world. No surprise there. All of his competitors—as well as Implements itself—are run by former accountants. These manufacturing executives demand, and get, obedience from their employees. Their companies are rigid and centralized; in short, the epitome of the world that is dying.

Airline serviettes have never been put to better use. We outlined to Larry our view of the new world filled with molecules, all of which have the customer at the nucleus. It was a fast-paced, no-obligation sales pitch to interest him and pass the time. We didn't need to bother. He was already there. There was great excitement on both sides. The plane landed and we exchanged cards. I'll call you sometime in the new year. No, you can't do anything for me now. I have everything I need. A hurried handshake.

Three months later, the phone rang. "Hi, I'm Jeff Roth from Implements, Inc. Larry asked me to give you a call."

INSIDE THE CHANGE PROCESS

Jeff Roth, vice president of human resources, came to the point quickly, as he sat in Implements' cafeteria.

"Our problem is we're so damn polite," he began, staring through his thick glasses. "We don't seem to be able to talk about the real issues. We've got a lot of shit to get on the table."

Although he was groping for words, there was no doubting his sincerity.

"I don't want you to advertise this, but, frankly we have some major problems here," he continued, involuntarily lowering his voice and glancing about the dining room, even though he had chosen a deserted corner to begin with. "Some of the people on the senior management team can't stand each other. They've been working together over thirty years and can't stand being in the same room. If Bill Humphrey comes into a meeting, likely as not Joe Dickson will walk out.

"Then there's the conflict between the new guys and the old guard. Larry Willatt has been here three years, and he brought a couple of us over with him. We're seen as Larry's men, and, truth to tell, we are. The others? Well, none of them has less than twenty years with the company. Most have never worked for anyone else. We have."

Jeff came to the company after spending some time in the financial services business. He had been with a couple of companies that had failed or had been merged out of existence. As the vice president for human resources, he had been the last man out the door each time, but it had been his job to fire the rest.

"Larry and I have been pushing change within the company, but we've run into a brick wall. There's no teamwork at the top. Did I show you the corporate culture study we had done? No? Let me get you a copy."

Implements had hired an organizational behavior consulting firm to come in and study its culture a few months back. The results were damning.

"Basically, they said we were the perfect company for the 1950s," Jeff said accurately. "It's like we knew that, but we don't know what to do about it." Jeff shrugged his shoulders and then sighed. "I've tried everything I can think of to get them to change, we've even tried Outward Bound. We'd have been better with 'Golfward Bound'; at least they would have been enthusiastic about that. The resistance they put up is unbelievable. Joe Dickson, the head of finance, simply won't take part in anything that smells of behavior training. And, the others treat any exercises designed to foster team building or change as a ridiculous waste of time.

"We need some way of breaking through. If we don't get it, we're finished."

It was clear that Jeff Roth and Larry felt the need to change. It was also clear that Larry was not going to get to his Molecular vision if he could not get even basic team cooperation in his top management group.

Did the others feel the need to change? we asked.

"I think so," Jeff answered. "We've been under incredible pressure for a while. There have been regulatory changes. Larry has been leading the charge on that. He must be spending two thirds of his time on regulatory issues. That's part of the problem. He's not around enough and the others aren't leaders yet. They don't know what to do—except carry on in the same old ways. But they have seen the numbers, and heard the talk about selling us. I think they will come around."

THE REAL WORK BEGINS

We started work with the premise that the company would not be sold. If Larry and his team sat around wondering what might happen, once the division was sold, nothing would get done.

After talking with Larry, we decided that our approach would be straightforward. We would present the business problem the company was facing, work with senior management to adjust the vision and structure of the company in order to obtain market success, then roll things out so the bulk of the people could adjust to the new environment.

Our goal was to get members of the management team to discuss the business objectively. If we could get them talking to one another, we figured we could get them to dispel the number one source of tension and misunderstanding. There is a tremendous lack of knowledge in most businesses about what everyone in the company does. In most organizations, the people are so split up and the walls between them so great that they are profoundly ignorant of each other's problems. If you don't know what someone does, you're bound to resent them. But since you don't want to be openly hostile, you keep your distance and smile a lot.

It's a condition we call "terminal politeness." People survive by not throwing rocks at each other—in public. In the end, the business collapses because its problems are too important and sensitive to talk about.

Once we got people talking, it was easy to hear their pain. Bill Humphrey has been with the company for over thirty years. From his position as the head of sales he has a good overview of the kinds of stress that everyone in the company has been under. He makes very clear how he feels: betrayed.

"The day they announced we were really for sale, a little bit of each of us died," he explained. "Were we angry? You bet. It's all very well being sold because you and your colleagues have failed. But to be sold to provide capital—like something at a secondhand sale—well, that just makes you feel sick."

He pauses, then adds: "Of course, there's no one really out there to buy us, and besides, I don't think that they would really sell us without our consent."

Denial is common in situations like this. So is the wistfulness.

"We were doing so well. We'd had our problems. Who doesn't? But we'd got the arithmetic right. We were starting to get at our cultural problems. We have some really good ideas. Ideas so revolutionary, we could stand this industry on its head. We could do it, you know. But the sale hanging over us took all the starch out of us. You had all these buyers parading through here. It's like showing a potential house buyer your underwear drawer. They want to see it all. You can't blame them, really. But it's a most disconcerting feeling. It's voyeurism, really. With some of them, you know they're asset strippers. They're looking for a deal. Sharks. No, vultures, really."

Bill's disgust, subsequently indicated by every other senior manager, plainly showed through. But so did the fear.

"Most of our managers have been here so long they wouldn't know how to find another job," Bill told us. "Mother looked after us. We're well paid. We were here for life. We've been spared so far, but did you know that in this part of the country 35 percent of the managers lost their jobs in the last two years? The people are afraid."

Back to the "might-of-beens."

"We've gotten a lot of autonomy in the last couple of years. Plus, they gave us a stable president. For nearly fifteen years, we've had revolving presidencies. They'd put a guy in here for two years, as a sort of finishing school, before they brought him back to corporate for a 'serious' senior job.

"So we had this bizarre situation. The best and brightest were sent here. But while they were here, they couldn't afford to do anything controversial. They had to keep their noses clean. They weren't going to do anything that would endanger that job back at corporate.

"Pre–Larry Willatt we were sliding down the slope. We hadn't done the job in keeping up with the changes in the industry. We were incredibly slow to respond to the invasion of the imports. And as a result of this, we kept dropping every time someone ranked the sales leaders in our industry. Our one big decision, to open a chain of retail stores to supplement our wholesale business, was a disaster. We didn't know the first thing about retailing, and all we did was alienate our traditional customers. Amidst all this, the parent didn't seem worried; we were hardly a blip on their radar screen. The decision to sell, although it had been rumored for some time, was devastating."

CULTURAL HANGOVER

Peter Dokes, the head of marketing planning, could describe perfectly what was wrong with Implements:

"We were used to being told what to do. We're a classic disempowered bureaucracy. As we've tried to change, to become more responsive to keep up with changes in the marketplace, we've got totally disoriented. We've tried to go from a company that was highly measured and highly autocratic to one that was highly empowered. You can imagine all the problems that has caused.

"In the past the answers to everything used to be in the manual," he continued. "You followed whatever was written down, and you couldn't go wrong. Now there are no answers in the back of the book. We can execute programs, and deliver products, as long as someone tells us what to do. If they don't, we're lost."

Part of the reason Implements was lost, Dokes had correctly realized, was that there was no communication between different parts of the company.

"During the coffee breaks, whenever we have a company-wide meeting, the functional groups stay together," he continued. "Larry is the only one who mingles. There's lots of 'turfdom' when some of the turf shouldn't even be there! Even in marketing we don't work together. There is a lot of

hoarding of information. We've been working on process improvement, trying to get more efficient, but our culture is working against us. All the dialogue has been defensive, protective. They'll tell you that you can't do this or that without their approval. We have rules and regulations for everything, all based on the assumption that the company knows best. You don't have to think for yourself. Indeed, no one wants you to think for yourself. We're rigid. Rule-driven. Safe. So out of touch with the real world. People here are rewarded for conformity and administrative skill. We've squeezed out all the creativity, and our halfhearted periodic attempts at empowerment have just confused things.

"I suppose given the way the business has been run you can't blame people for the fact that no one really cares about their job," Peter added. "If you look out the window at four-fifteen, you'd see there's a line up to get out of the parking lot. We work six hours a day."

One of the first things you learn in interviewing people is not to be afraid of the silences. If you don't rush in to ask another question, usually the person being interviewed will feel compelled to fill the void. That's what happened here. We let the silence run, and Peter continued with perhaps a bit more candor than before. What we heard was a man in love with his company, seeing what appeared to be insurmountable problems and fearing the chaos. The words began tumbling out, and he doubled back to some of what he had just told us, as if to underscore the points.

"We're stodgy. The people feel they're protected. The trade-off for that is we don't give people the authority to make decisions. No wonder they don't feel accountable. We never rewarded them for being responsible or accountable. Our bonus plan is ridiculous. If you're doing poorly, you won't get a 4 percent increase, only 3.5 percent. Really good performance earns 4.2 percent! Do you want to know how bad things are? Our profit-sharing is based on seniority.

"Empowerment was to change all that. We cut the organization strings, and suddenly everything seemed to go the other way. People were told to do their own thing. It really frightened the older managers. Things started to become uncoordinated.

"Look, I've gone on long enough. It all boils down to this. We have fundamental skill problems. We're implementers but not self-starters. We lack strategic skills. We can't get a product out the door. We don't think about the business aspects of a problem."

NOW WHAT?

Three views become painfully clear after all the senior managers have had a chance to talk. The executives are either cynical, hopeful or dismissive. None of these views are particularly promising. The common theme that is emerging is that the psychologists who had come in to evaluate the firm were right. This is a very "old world" company.

One quick example will drive home the point. When we asked managers at the company what it would take to succeed at Implements, Inc., here is what they told us:

- **Don't rock the boat.**
- **Don't be late.**
- **Do what you're told.**
- **Cover your butt.**
- **Always agree.**
- **Don't say what you really think.**

Changing Implements, Inc., wasn't going to be easy. That was something that Larry Willatt and Jeff Roth understood.

"We need a burning platform to shock the people out of their torpor. Otherwise nothing is going to change," Jeff said.

"But, a burning platform is exactly what we haven't got," Larry said. "We're coming out of one of our most profitable years. We gave out some of the highest bonuses in corporate history. Why would anybody think we would have to change?"

The reasons were obvious if you weren't stuck looking at the trees. Implements was slow to market with new products, steadily losing share as everyone else expanded far quicker. And the company was anything but customer responsive.

But that was the view from the outside. It was obvious that few inside the company had a true sense of what was going on.

Larry continued, talking more to himself than to us: "There is a theory that the only way to shake up an organization is to execute a few enemies of state. I don't subscribe to that. I believe that the bulk of the problems result from the way things are done, rather than from bad people. This isn't to say you can't have too much structure. But shooting people to make a point isn't my style."

Jeff Roth picked up on his theme of a burning platform as if Larry had never spoken.

"I think the enemy is within. I think our people are scared that they won't be able to change, that they won't be able to adapt to a new way of doing business," he said. "That fear is real—and justified. We're going to have to deal with it openly. In the last two years I cannot recall an open, honest conversation about any of the critical issues facing the business, because people are afraid they are going to say something that is going to ruin their careers. We avoid issues, and walk out of a management meeting and do the opposite of what we've just agreed to. There isn't honesty between individuals, no commitment to each other, no appreciation of each other's contribution."

Larry didn't disagree with a thing that Jeff said, and that just underscored how hard changing the company would be.

EARLY BUMPS

The management committee is crammed into a basement room at a luxury hotel near Implements' headquarters. The heating system is cranked up to high, making the room unpleasant, and things don't improve as they hear the results of the interviews.

People listen attentively and Joe Dickson, vice president of finance, expresses what every Implements manager is thinking: "We know all this. It's like the corporate culture stuff all over again. It's a good mirror of who we are. But what are we going to do about it?"

What they needed to do was listen to new voices, people within the company who had a different perspective, and a different point of view. They needed to include people at lower levels of the company in their discussions.

You could have cut the tension with a knife once that suggestion was made. We could not have chosen a more explosive issue. The management committee, as various members had made clear during our interviews, had difficulty agreeing. Expose their behavior to a wider audience and it would be the equivalent of revealing the Emperor had no clothes. Plus, Implements, Inc., was built on intense hierarchy. To have lower ranking people in the meeting would be a major break with tradition. All of this was conveyed to us in an overlapping rush of voices.

There was prolonged protest, but eventually—grudgingly—they accepted the fact that they should let new peo-

ple into the group, if for no other reason than to send a message that this time would be different. After a silence that seemed to stretch forever, Bill Humphrey, the head of sales, decided to speak first.

"All right, if that is the way we're going to go, I need my three guys in here. Arthur, Peter, Jack." More silence, but you can sense what everyone else is thinking, sales is now overrepresented.

Joe Dickson, the head of finance, says, "And I need Frank and Jim." Two MBAs are clearly worth more than three salesmen.

The debate freezes, nobody else is sure if they should commit their people. Eventually someone decides to appeal to the boss.

"Larry, what do you want?"

"I think I want you to decide."

The pain was visible on all nine faces in the room. They had handled the problem of how many people should be in the room as they had handled every other problem in their past, with politeness and an attempt to reach a compromise. But here politeness wasn't working, and there didn't seem to be a compromise. They would actually have to make a decision.

They finally did. The group was increased to fifteen. Meetings would be held off-site, and they would do their best to try to change.

At the end of the session we sat down with Larry to talk through where we were at—as we would at the end of all the sessions.

"I don't think even I realized how far we had to go" was Larry's opening remark. "I think my claim that we were on our way to a Molecular Organization may have been a little exaggerated!" The product of wishful thinking—yes. But, all leadership starts with a vision, and we would see if Larry's could be made to happen.

A THOUGHT REVOLUTION

Déjà vu all over again. Another basement room in a classy but discreet conference hotel. Fifteen men in the room, together for the first time to discuss the future of their business. They look around, shy and surprised.

They've never really been forced to spend any amount of time together before.

Larry welcomes the new members, introduces us, and we get up to go to work.

"OK, let's get started. Strategy begins with two simple questions: Who's the customer? What do they value?"

The group sinks back in their chairs. This is going to be easy. The customer is the end user.

Well, maybe not, someone says. What about the dealer? And what about the government clients? Then there's purchasing, of course. They break up into small groups to figure out who exactly they should be serving.

Two and a half hours later they reassemble, and to the surprise of almost everyone in the room, they had all agreed on the same customer: the dealer.

They spend some time exploring how they came to this decision. It turns out the ultimate relationship with the end user is between the customer and the dealer, not between the end user and Implements. There is no way to gain a competitive advantage with the end user, because it is almost impossible to differentiate the product.

The insight may have been basic, but it would turn the company on its head. Decades of treating the dealer as the enemy—as someone who stood between Implements and the end user—would have to go by the wayside. It will be difficult, but the consensus is that it is the right thing to do.

All in all, an extremely productive morning. We head to lunch.

Over salad and éclairs, the personalities of the group start

emerging. Arthur Dace, who runs sales distribution, was pleased with the results of the morning session. He had believed all along that the dealer was the customer. But it was clear that he was skeptical about the group's decision to come around to his point of view. "They'll [referring to the rest of the management group] never be able to stick with the idea that the dealer is the customer. Our culture is too ingrained in its assumptions about the dealer."

Later, during lunch, Jeff Roth said the same thing. "Don't get me wrong, I think focusing on the dealer is right," he began. "But it is too big a cultural leap for us, too threatening to too many people. It would mean hundreds of jobs lost. It means that we will have to shift many of the things we have back at headquarters out into the field or turn it over to the dealers."

The more they talk, the more they convince themselves that the dealer really isn't the customer. A focal point, perhaps, but not the customer.

That sets off Arthur Dace, whose primary job is satisfying Implements' dealer network. He literally starts to yell, and you get the feeling that several years of frustration are being released.

"You guys don't understand the sales force or the dealers or what they are capable of doing," he begins. "You don't know what the dealers are capable of; you have never tried to find out." He stops as quickly as he began, shoulders hunched in frustration.

Larry steps in in an attempt to get a discussion of the real issues going.

"Arthur, why don't you tell us about the distributors," he begins. "What qualifications do they have? How have they changed over the years? Maybe, everyone is a little out of date with what is going on."

And so the first hesitant sharing of information began. It turns out that things really had changed among the dealers,

who had always been seen as not-too-bright high school graduates. Today, Arthur explained, half of them are now college graduates with basic business skills, looking to expand their business. They would need less hand-holding than we would have thought.

Perhaps the dealers could carry the business, everyone agreed.

Knowing that the dealer is the customer is a beginning. It gives the group a flag to rally around. They spend the next day refining that idea into a fourteen-word vision statement: "We will be the leader in helping dealers develop extraordinary relationships with their customers."

They have established a proposition: "We are here to serve the customer." And they have selected that customer, the dealer. Everything builds on top of that. The more they build the new vision of their company, the more they will own it, and it will become unthinkable to go backwards.

By mid-afternoon of the second day, they have a final vision statement: "We will provide all the necessary tools and resources that will enable our dealers to develop and sustain extraordinary relationships with their customers that will give those customers peace of mind."

Everyone buys in. Success. Everyone is now united around who the customer is and how Implements should serve him or her. Slowly, very slowly, the group is coming together. In the course of two days they have agreed on two separate, but vital, issues. Will this continue? The "team," such as it is, has a reputation for doing its own thing, once it leaves the meeting.

Our chat with Larry is much more positive. "I wouldn't have believed after the first session that we could get any agreement out of them," he remarks, clearly relieved. "Perhaps we are getting the team together after all."

Sorry to deflate his hopes, but we have made only the very first tentative steps along the road to either understand-

ing the customer or creating teamwork. But we did get off the ground.

THE DOWNER

This time the group meets in the country at another hotel, one with a golf course on the grounds. But we are still in a basement. We are beginning to think that there must be something significant about basements. Every meeting so far has been underground. We are expecting a downer of a meeting. It is normal. They have had a chance to convince themselves that the agreements last time didn't happen and they really can't change.

The aim is to get them past that by forcing them to work on lots of detail about the business and its environment and competition, to get them to tap into their knowledge and to broaden the conversation to get them used to talking together. The hope is, by drawing on the skills that each of them has, the group will be able to find new opportunities within its market.

It sounds great. And then Larry Willatt blows it.

His group lets him lead the discussion. Even worse, he takes the pen and stands at the flip chart. Real dominance. But what is worse is that his group lets him dominate. They don't interrupt even when it is clear that his stream-of-consciousness talk about potential opportunities in the industry is vague at best and totally contradictory at worst. He's the boss, their body language says. This should be interesting. If it's not, well, he's the boss. They listen and don't interrupt.

The groups come back to the basement. Larry presents first. He gives a rambling incoherent explanation about what Implements should be doing.

The second group gets up. The presenter, Joe Dickson,

turns to the room. "Well, now to actually answer the question."

Everyone looks at Larry. How will he take it?

Larry just nods and laughs. He knows he blew it. Tension disperses. Antagonism becomes friendly rivalry, the boss has shown his mettle as a leader. The group shares the laughs and is closer than it has ever been. We finish on a high.

"This is some roller coaster!" Larry, a good sport as ever, is rueful about his mistakes. But the fact is, he had some major gains. They have bought in to some basic ideas—that the market is fragmented, that the dealer is still the customer and that sharing knowledge is a valuable activity. We are beginning to chip away at terminal politeness.

THE LEAP

The same hotel. The same people. The same basement. Time to explore the work implications of the vision and to talk about real threats and real opportunities that may result from our time together. The group that is meeting here—nearly six months after our work began—is very different than the one we met twenty-three weeks ago. They are used to the process; they're more relaxed and they have begun exchanging information.

As they enter the room, there are tiny flickers of hope. They have stuck with the idea of having the company revolve around the dealer. Goodwill in the group is growing.

The question this time is simple: Given the vision, what are the key capabilities that the team must put in place to make it happen?

It is a crucial question. Whatever answers they come up with will end up structuring what the company will look like from here on out. Everything, from what the quality program will look like to how the information system will

function, depends on the answer. This will be a major strategic planning decision for people not used to thinking broadly.

There are hours of discussion. This is their world. They can't talk about it enough. But their thinking is as we feared: all over the place. It's like a shaggy rug. It's going to have to be pulled together.

The group comes back together and begins talking to see if it can move toward consensus. The starting point is parts. How should that division be handled?

Jack, head of parts, starts to get defensive immediately. The consensus is that all the problems Implements has with its parts department—continually having too much inventory, being slow to ship out replacements and having a high number of accidents among the drivers—can all be solved, or eliminated, if we move to a just-in-time system.

Jack instantly counterattacks. "Everyone always attacks parts," he says. "We're doing a terrific job. The people work hard and all they get is abuse. If you push it out to the dealers, the entire system will fall apart. No one understands the work that's been done. If I tell what you are planning to do to my people they'll quit."

Silence. Then Peter swings into the attack. The parts division is costing the company money. Larry quickly cuts him off.

"Let's look at what we have," he begins. "It's a possible idea. No one is suggesting a wholesale massacre of the parts department. It's at the core of the business. Who knows what the final answer will be? You, Jack, and your people are the ones who have to create the answer, not the group in this room. That's the only way the change process works, with people reinventing their own work. This group just sets context and provides a list of questions that have to be answered."

Nods of agreement. Now to spread the pain. "Everyone

will have to rethink their world," Larry continues. "Technology and the marketplace will demand it. What that means, Jack, is that you're not alone." Soothing words. No point in antagonizing Jack, the company needs him, and he's an important part of the future.

Jack begins to calm down. He has made his point and it has been acknowledged if not accepted.

We step back in to see if we can drive them to a search for a final synthesis. "What we are creating here is a new company, a company where all the key functions will be dispersed into the marketplace and placed in the hands of the people who deal directly with the customers, your dealers. Your key issue will be the management of that dispersed system."

There are nods of agreement all around, and Larry Willatt is delighted. This is basically the vision he shared with us on the plane ride a year ago. Arthur Dace loves it. Intellectually, he will tell you it makes a lot of sense, but since he is also the head of distribution, the decision makes him the biggest winner within the company. Jack Park is not yet happy and remains quiet. Bill Humphrey, the head of sales, looks lost.

"I thought I knew what we were heading toward," Bill says. "We were going to think about shifting more of the responsibility out into the field. But there's been an afterburner placed on the idea. I don't recognize it anymore." It seems like a good time to break for coffee.

We have bumped up against a major problem. An idea, in this case the boss's vision, has suddenly been exposed. People are surprised and now they feel there was a hidden agenda. There is only one answer—to address the issue directly.

After the break we walk through the chain of logic again and Larry explains it in detail. He expresses how his vision of the dispersed organization has been around for a long time.

It was always inherent in his remarks about information systems as well as in a hundred other things he had said. All that had happened was that they had come to the same conclusion. Gradually, logic overcame any objections and people started to relate to the new image.

We still have one major issue left to resolve. It is time to spread the word on what they have decided. It will be done through a series of meetings. The question is who will attend. They create a preliminary list, and it is clear that power and departmental politics have not gone away; everyone argues to have their departments overrepresented. But unlike six months ago, the issue is resolved quickly. The key criteria they use in deciding who will be invited is who will be helpful in communicating the idea through the company. A group of sixty is decided upon, and the senior management group leaves the hotel on a high.

They now have a new image of the business and a clearly defined goal of where they are heading. How far they have come as a team is clear: They actually talk to one another during coffee breaks, and they are open, trying to understand the business issues facing each other.

Our conversation with Larry focused on the shift in image. "It had to happen," he says. "They were bound to be surprised. They were so wrapped up in thinking the old way that the new idea springing out like that was sure to be a shock." Larry hit the key problem of a leader at this stage of a change—his sole vision hits his desire to create team consensus. His solution is the only viable one. If he had ducked the challenge and said that this was only one among many options, he would never get the team focused on a new way of doing business. His show of determination and support for the new concept was crucial. As they saw it, they were forced to either accept or reject. By then treating the issue as a logical outcome of their own thinking, he was able to gain acceptance.

SPREADING THE WORD

Another large resort, but this one comes complete with memories. It is here that senior management retreats every year to discuss strategy and play golf. It has always been by invitation only, and attendance has always been based on hierarchy. But this time, much of the senior management isn't present. It's sixty people from various levels within the company. Inviting a mixed group of sixty here has a deep symbolic significance about what the new world at Implements, Inc., will be all about. Back in the city are some seriously worried and bruised egos.

They listen to a summary of the interviews from the first small group session. What did they think? They're shocked. They hadn't thought top management understood the problem. This is a common reaction, one that helps form a basis of trust among the people assembled.

With common ground established, we divide them up into teams. We are going to begin, we tell them, with a discussion of the vision and what it means to have the dealer as their customer. But first some ground rules. You don't have to agree just because it is your boss's vision, but you'll have to be able to defend your disagreement.

After six hours of discussion, they have materially improved the vision statement: "We will revolutionize the delivery of our products and services by providing the tools and resources that will enable our dealers to develop extraordinary relationships that give their customers peace of mind."

They have taken the original vision statement, honed it and pushed it further than their managers did.

When top management hears the vision, they are surprised, but they shouldn't have been. The middle-level managers in the company were not incompetent. They understood what was going on in the marketplace and many of them had come to the decision long ago that the company needed to be focused around the dealer. They knew what needed to be done, but no one had asked them.

Also, organizing around the dealer wasn't a new idea. That Larry and some of his senior staff had been thinking this way had been known for some time. There are very few secrets in a company. The employees had time to absorb the idea.

Or had they? Was this just another example of the old hierarchy reasserting itself? Were they just agreeing because that's what the boss wanted them to do? No one will ever know for sure, but it was probably untainted agreement.

That resolved, it is time to address the issue of changing Implements' culture. The senior group had been focusing virtually exclusively on business strategy. There had been some early discussion about values and culture, but not much.

The responsibility to define and change the culture on the shoulders of the large group was before us now. It would be their job to decide how the human dynamics should evolve and what would be needed to get the message out and make it stick. That the top team should hand off something as fundamental as this represented a dramatic shift.

In presenting the document, which stressed the need for openness and full communication at (and between) all levels of the company, the group made it clear that they were producing this set of values for management to review and polish but not to reinvent. The revolution had begun.

The large team meeting was finishing as a major triumph. All objectives were met. And Larry was beginning to feel the onrush of a Molecular Organization. But we were not so sure. We were convinced that there was all kinds of goodwill but it was still untested. Making a shift as fundamental as this in a very traditional company was going to demand some tough people decisions. We needed to test the mettle of the top team and their willingness to take tough choices. It was time for the "burning platform." Larry agreed to go off and do some new arithmetic.

CHANGE BY THE NUMBERS

Everybody was still on a high when they arrived for the next meeting of senior management. We were in an "in town" hotel, and for the first time, we weren't in the basement. The people were in good spirits. This session was billed as about values—easy stuff, everyone thought.

We began by giving them an image to work with. Change is a journey. Making the journey is like building a bridge from where you were to the place where you see yourself. You build that bridge as you cross it, and it stands on struts called values. You can't get to the new world using the old values. You must create and practice the new ones along the way.

In the course of the journey some people fall by the wayside. Others never set out. Still others drop off the bridge into an emotional swamp, from which they may or may not ever emerge.

Before setting out on the journey, you need to have a very clear idea of why you are leaving home. There must be a totally compelling reason. If the house needs a bit of tinkering, you do it and stay home. Only if the house cannot be renovated do you tear it down to rebuild.

Before we can discuss values, we all need to agree that there is a need to leave home. We must agree that the new world, when we get there, will be the right world. We must understand the stresses we will be under along the way.

Today is the day we decide to leave home. Today is the day we look at the financials.

Two hours later, the shock was beginning to settle in.

Larry had done some arithmetic. He had taken the trends in the industry and projected them out three years. Three years is about as long as changing Implements should take. He drew us a picture of today and a picture of tomorrow. Then the question was: Can Implements achieve the economics of tomorrow by adapting what we have today? If it was possible to achieve future economics today, then changing Implements would be close to impossible. The need to renovate the existing house would overwhelm everything else. But if it was not possible to achieve future economics today, then it might be possible to get everyone to agree on the level of change that was necessary.

For the first time Larry put numbers behind the hunch that had been driving him to follow through with the change process. He had been convinced from day one that Implements' cost structure was far too high and the only way the company could achieve success was by dramatic change.

He stood up in front of the group and slowly went through the numbers. After four hours of discussion, there was clearly no alternative other than radically changing the company. Up to one third of the cost structure would have to go—that was a very polite way of saying that one out of every three jobs would disappear. To lessen the shock, the group set up a task force to clarify the numbers, but no one expected anything different. It was a sad group that went home that night.

In anticipation of this problem, Jeff Roth had hired a new person for his staff, Joanne Herriot. We quickly started calling her our "Betazoid," referring to the Counselor Troi on *Star Trek: The Next Generation*. Betazoids, on the television show, are advisers who sense human emotions in stressful situations. Joanne made an interesting barometer of the stress in the room.

As the meeting went on, and it became clear that the company had to be much smaller, she had to move away from the table. First she stood halfway back in the room, then in the back of the room, and finally she had to go out to her car and scream. She was used to one-on-one situations. The cumulative stress on the management group overwhelmed her.

As Jeff Roth left that evening, he was in a deep depression. He had wanted to bring to the surface all the issues that were holding back Implements, but the results were too brutal for him. He went home to a sleepless night. Before we left, we tried to figure out how to pick up the pieces.

By eight-thirty the following morning, all of them were back in their chairs, partially resigned to the inevitable. While significantly reducing the workforce would not be easy, there was at least a blueprint to follow that could minimize the pain. They had a vision. They knew where they wanted to take the company, and they knew, thanks to the work they had done, that they would have to get there by relying on the values they had set for themselves: openness, team work and integrity.

Looking back at the values that the large group had produced, we noticed that two leapt off the page: pushing down responsibility and decision making, and being open and honest with the people. As they wrestled with what those meant, they started to understand that the change process, with its potential for helping people reinvent their jobs, was the best way of getting at the problem of figuring out which jobs should go. That led to a discussion of not only who the company valued, but what. Eventually, the discussion moved on to the concept of integrity.

Integrity is perhaps one of the slipperiest of concepts.

And this debate proved it. Basically the discussion centered around how the senior managers at Implements could act with integrity and still keep secrets from the organization. Some secrets were obviously necessary, but wouldn't they be betraying trust if they withheld information? They were getting bogged down, so we provided them with insights we had gleaned from our work with other companies.

What people are really concerned about when they talk about a lack of integrity is a violation of their sense of justice and equity. What offends them is inequality when it comes to how decisions are made. In the case of reducing the number of jobs, they didn't mean that each department should lose the same amount of people. People expect their leaders to lead and make the tough decisions. And if that meant entire departments should be eliminated, so be it. But the integrity meant here must be a solid business reason behind the decision. The decision of which jobs would be lost would have to be based on market considerations, not individual advantage, in order to be seen as fair.

The situation is compounded when concerns about integrity are mixed up with compensation. For example, should senior managers be allowed to stay over in the hotel after a session for an extra night so they can get in a day of golf, and then charge the whole thing to the company? The discussion played off those points, and within fifteen minutes the group was having the basic discussions they needed to have about trust and their roles in achieving it. A major breakthrough.

Larry was calm but flushed as the sessions ended. He knew he had taken a major step. If he was to go back now, his leadership credibility would be shot. But the way forward was full of pain. To his credit he stuck with it—after all, the numbers had spoken. A tough few weeks followed as the numbers were thrashed over.

And thrashed over they were. But they always told the same story. It was a sadder but toughened top team that took on the rest of the change.

THE END OF UNCERTAINTY

Finally, the group got the word it was hoping for. The company was taken off the block. There would be no sale. The relief was tangible.

And now it was time to put pressure on Larry. From the beginning he had refused structural and personnel changes until the sale was over. As the sale negotiations continued, he had become increasingly disengaged from the business. He worked on regulatory issues and took to serving on other boards of directors. It was as if he had put himself in a kind of emotional limbo. People had noticed and broadly understood and did not press him on it.

Until now. They asked him to live up to his word about making changes once the fate of the division was known, and he did. Discussions were held and retirement packages were prepared for three executives, each of whom had expressed a wish to go. Other responsibilities were realigned and the expensive top management structure started to come into line with the economics of the business.

The slimmed-down group now started to really take ownership of the change. They still had team problems, and will have for a long time, as they have so much history to live with. But the terminal politeness is over, and they operate as a group. The vision and business strategy for the future were taken to the big group again and totally accepted. They now owned it and rolled it out to the rest of the company.

Larry felt vindicated. "I always felt we could get there, and now that we are looking past personalities and dealing with the realities of the business, I am sure we will get there." And they will. They are rapidly heading through Stage 2—the technology exploration—and are already attacking the management system to loosen it up.

STAGE 1 GOLDEN RULES

• Always start with the customer

The decision about who the customer is and on which level (consumer, intermediary, etc.) you are going to focus, in the hope of gaining competitive advantage, is pivotal to change. All customers must be served, but organizations can only find advantage with one level of customer. Forcing a decision as to who the customer is not only gives you strategic focus, it creates a precedent for agreement at a very early stage in the change process. In organizations with total product focus, like Implements, Inc., taking even this first step can yield groundbreaking insight on the nature of the business.

• Liftoff burns incredible energy

Getting a rocket ten feet off the ground uses up most of the fuel of a launch. The same is true of a change. In stagnant companies with no sense of a need to change, the pressure on the leader is enormous. However, without a clear felt need to change nothing will happen. The result is a delicate balancing act of pressing the team but ensuring that they buy into the vision at their own pace with the knowledge that they have the opportunity to mold its development. Regardless, if the leader doesn't drive on, the whole process will collapse.

• An end to terminal politeness
Terminal politeness is a common disease of companies like Implements, Inc. The solution to it is talking and talking and talking. The accumulated ignorance of years of separation by functional walls is often profound. In these early stages just getting the group talking—about the customer and then the business—is a triumph. However, the talk has to be real. People who persist in the old behavior have to be called on it as the group starts to mature.

WCI America—Life After Quality

Most companies are less than a few decades old, so they are "wet behind the ears" when it comes to change. Not so for World Communications Interna- tional (WCI). The company has been in business for over a hundred years and has had to reinvent itself many times in order to move with the prevailing tech- nologies.

During the 1980s, WCI America (as WCI is called in both North and South America) was a boom com- pany, expanding into the information technology world providing communication and information ser- vices to a wide range of industries. However, an in- tense recession and the introduction of even more fierce competition forced it to change once again. The key this time is to recognize that resistance is inevitable when you try to change an organization. The secret is to use that resistance as a positive force for change.

WCI America (WCIA) represents a remarkable example of an organization making a successful transition to Stage 2. This transformation shows the tremendous emotional effort and leadership strength needed to overcome powerful resistance to culture change.

"We tried 'quality' two years ago. I really believed it was a good idea," sighed Jeff Wilson, president of WCI America (WCIA). "We had consultants in and really got going. We pulled out all the stops and formed a bunch of teams, and while there were the usual naysayers, we persisted and made a lot of progress for the first eight or nine months."

Before the quality program was in place, it often took WCIA five weeks to get a customer up and running. After the program had been implemented, it only took a week and the technician did the job right the first time. Previously, he would have to make four or five service calls before the client was happy. Jeff believed that the organization had to get out of its own way so that a highly talented workforce could get on with the job of serving the customer.

Things initially went well, but "then we got lost in the woods, with all those teams, and endless flow charts of our business operations," Wilson continued. Teams were created for the sake of teams and, while some made progress, there was no orderly way to share the learning with others. People kept solving the same problems again and again. "Quality Comes First!" posters popped up everywhere but there was no follow-through. More importantly, while quality by any objective standard had improved, the quality program didn't really address the real problems that were plaguing WCIA.

During the 1980s, the information revolution came to our desks and to our homes. As improvements in satellites and fiber optics came into play, the explosion of computing capability and the leap in communications attracted hordes of competitors—some big, some small. Each tried to outdo the other in value-added services to the increasingly sophisticated customer. WCIA was in there struggling, but the company was losing market share and profits. All the effort put on the quality program seemed almost peripheral to these big threats.

That left people frustrated. "Did we do something wrong in implementing the quality program?" they asked themselves repeatedly. And the news that WCIA was bringing in another set of consultants didn't make them feel much better. They had worked hard on the quality program. In fact they had thought they were doing a good job even before there was a formal quality program. Why did they have to go through all of this again?

The story was a familiar one. We have seen many situations where these types of programs get off to a good start. After all, improving quality no matter what your business is a good idea. The problem is that the process of implementing the changes to support the idea can quickly mushroom. Suddenly, you have a dozen groups, all going off in different directions, and it is not surprising that some of them end up getting lost in the weeds.

Traditionally, when people think about quality, they concentrate on the throughput—what the company ends up selling in the marketplace. The problem is they tend to ignore everything else. If it takes three days for a package to get out of the mailroom, or the lawyers aren't brought in until the product is ready to roll (which delays the shipping date by three weeks), an organization's quality is affected as well.

These were the sort of things that were bogging down WCIA and making it slow to respond to changes in the marketplace. After the first quality program stalled, Jeff and a group from the senior management team went out to study other companies that had successfully gone through major changes to try to learn what WCIA had done, and was doing, wrong.

A trip to Milliken, the U.S. textile firm, convinced Jeff and his team that the effort was worth another shot. Milliken had bounced back from oblivion and out-Japanesed the Japanese through team building, quality circles, implementing employee suggestions and turning managers into coaches. The management team wasn't sure that was the route that WCIA should take, but they were extremely impressed with the results.

Specifically, they were fascinated by the overwhelming commitment to change and continuous improvement at all levels of the organization at Milliken from the president down to the shop floor. Everyone was so involved in the transformation of the business, and so full of energy. After seeing how manufacturing speed and just-in-time delivery systems made Milliken's customers dependent on them, Jeff and his team called us in and said they were convinced that real change was possible at WCIA.

So we were there as "Change Experts," not quality specialists. The problem, as the senior management saw it, was to resuscitate the quality program, but not to make the same mistakes WCIA had the first time around. The real challenge would be that we would only get one kick at the ball. When you blow something major, like a quality program, you face even more skepticism on the second go-round than you do on the first.

So WCIA was starting from a disadvantage. There was no real reason for people to buy into changing the company. The company had tried it once and then had backed away. Because of the earlier defeat, employees felt they could just lie low and wait until the next wave rolled over them.

DIAGNOSING THE PROBLEM

The first order of business was to figure out what the real problem was for WCIA. Quality is always important, but were quality problems a core issue, or simply a symptom of something else? When you go to the doctor and say, "My knee hurts," he could easily put a bandage on your knee, but that may not be what is really wrong with you. You might be experiencing referred pain from your back.

There is often another problem that is creating the symptom, and you have to get to the root cause. To do that, we began as we always do, by conducting in-depth interviews with dozens of key managers at all levels of the company in order to dig behind the surface issues.

WCI America represents a company that has had a string of successful products and services. What success often brings, however, is an inward focus—"we're the best!"—because major competitors have not yet appeared. Then things change and competition starts to make significant inroads in the market. Typically, the successful company wakes up late to this harsh reality.

The challenge was to get WCIA back to focusing on the customer—a Stage 2 transition issue. A major culture change was required that went beyond just having more exciting products, mobilizing every nook and cranny of the organization to "think customer."

As we began to learn more about the organization, three specific issues surfaced that had to be factored into our work:

- **A vicious new competitive environment.** The company had always been the recognized leader, and now not only was there more competition than ever before, but some of WCIA's competitors were getting ahead of them, creatively bundling new features and services with the product.
- **Interdepartmental/functional conflict.** People were talking and working at cross-purposes in different parts of the organization.
- **A struggle to reconcile growth with WCIA's roots.** Everyone in the organization agreed that the company had to move faster, and indeed it was moving faster than ever before. But with that increased speed came a longing, from many of the company's employees, for the simpler past where everyone knew everybody in the company, and you had a job for life once you joined the firm. They asked why you couldn't work in a fast-moving company that still had a family feeling.

Let's take them one at a time.

VICIOUS NEW COMPETITIVE ENVIRONMENT

Perhaps the most salient feature of WCIA's problem was that the late 1980s was accompanied by flat profits. Indeed, by the time we were called in, the company's profits had vanished. What made this situation worse was that WCI in Europe, arguably a much less competitive environment, was making a fortune.

WCI used to be about the only game in town, but now competition—especially in the United States—was tough and things weren't going to get easier any time soon.

The most advanced customers were increasingly using highly sophisticated systems in an attempt to stay ahead of the next guy. Niche competitors were starting to offer innovative features, including some catchy novelties. The appetite of the marketplace for hot new features was outstripping WCIA's ability to introduce fresh innovations. The company had been slow to respond and had been several years late on the promised delivery of new enhancements to the product line.

Product development reported directly to the European office, rather than to WCIA (in the interests of worldwide consistency), slowing down the whole process. Besides, the market in America, as anyone who worked at WCIA could tell you, had special needs. Things had to change.

INTERDEPARTMENTAL/FUNCTIONAL CONFLICT

You can't go into any organization larger than a dozen people and not find barriers between departments and even larger units within a company. WCI America was no different, but in WCIA's case we found that these barriers had a particular flavor.

First, the lion's share of product development was done out of Europe, the head office, and therefore wasn't controlled by WCIA at all. Being on the other side of the Atlantic from the American market made it hard for the home office to know exactly what kinds of products were needed. Not surprisingly, this led to a "we-they" attitude between headquarters and its American division, something, of course, that happens in any large organization. All of this divisiveness was reflected in some major product launch delays and in WCIA being slow to keep up with the market-place. Although Jeff Wilson himself was British, he was much more attuned to the American way of doing things.

Second, there was an ongoing battle between the sales department and the technology people. The impressive capability to service clients that had been built up in the 1980s felt in the 1990s like Gulliver tied down by the Lilliputians. The technology people's inflexibility triggered massive customer irritation. They constantly asked for information to be presented in ways that the technology simply could not handle.

Finally, the company had a major culture clash. The problems of the late 1980s after a decade of untrammeled growth brought the financial types out of the woodwork. The sales and service people may have disagreed about a lot of things, but they all knew that the finance people didn't understand the business and were killing it. As usual, this belief held more than a grain of truth. Jeff himself was a finance guy—an image that is hard to shake. And that brings us to the final point.

A STRUGGLE TO RECONCILE GROWTH WITH WCIA'S ROOTS

Echoing the sentiments of the people we interviewed, one person said wistfully that WCIA used to be "a very comfortable place, like a family. We not only knew each other's first names, but the names of their children."

Then WCI internationally got "BIG," riding on the info-tech explosion of that decade. The company went public in the mid-eighties. The once tiny firm grew into a high-tech global information dynamo by the time the decade was over. WCIA was a major part of this boom.

Hitting $1 billion in annual sales globally was nice, but

along with the growth came a change in the corporate culture. People in the office started saying, "Who's that?" as somebody walked by. More important, the old informal networks—the channels through which things really get done in any organization—broke down. In the past, you always knew who to call—"good old Bill" or "Susan"—if things were in a mess and you needed a little help. However, somehow during the boom, that individual was gone and nobody knew who had taken his or her place.

Organizations easily can become unhinged when they totally turn their backs on the past. On the other hand, constant change is necessary to remain competitive. What's WCIA—an organization that started as a family manufacturing firm in the nineteenth century—supposed to look like in the age of satellite links and computers? How do you reconcile the need for a family feeling in an age of high tech? The answer lies in creatively reinventing the best of the past in the light of new realities.

The point about reinvention was driven home to us many years ago, as we studied U.S. history. With the War of Independence, the United States proudly proclaimed "freedom of the individual" as a basic tenet for the new nation. What was actually meant, of course, was freedom for white, landowning males. With the advent of the Civil War, the principle of freedom for the individual was not abandoned but rather reinvented to include blacks. Later, by 1920, with the suffragette movement in full flower, it was expanded to include women. Today we have once again reinvented "freedom for the individual" to incorporate minorities, people with AIDS and others whose rights we feel must be upheld.

If this principle, so pivotal to the nation, had been thrown out when it first became obsolete, we would have lost a vital part of the American soul. That, of course, didn't happen. Instead, the principle was reinvented to reflect changing realities.

Reinventing a corporate culture has more to do with emotional baggage, egos and who did what to whom when than it does with hard-core business strategy. People are used to doing things a certain way and resist any change. After all, as humans, we are all creatures of habit. The emotional baggage in WCIA had a lot to do with the company's origins and the shared history of its employees.

The challenge in WCIA, then, was how to reach back inside the corporate psyche to find the part of its soul that had made it such an exciting place to be over the years and to reinvent it so the company could be exciting once again.

ENGAGING IN THE MOTHER OF ALL STRUGGLES

This is where we started: with a company that had achieved greatness, but was starting to lose its edge in the marketplace. In terms of trying to change WCIA's culture, there was good news and bad news. The good news was that the company was not sliding into bankruptcy; it had a moderate loss. Good because we had a little more room to maneuver. Bad because there was just no sense of urgency, no feeling that the company had to "change or else." As someone said, "Nothing focuses the mind like the fact that you are going to be hanged in the morning." Organizations in serious trouble don't have long internal debates about whether they need to change. They know they have no choice. Companies that are limping along just don't have the same compelling need.

As we considered our task ahead, we realized that one of our primary challenges would be to turn a great deal of skepticism—a natural phenomenon in companies where a program has died after being introduced with much fanfare as the company's savior—into useful, focused energy. We couldn't paint over the skepticism or ignore it. That's what ultimately sank the quality program the first time around—people stopped believing in management's commitment to the idea. We would have to deal with it.

Over the years, we have come to realize that skepticism can be used in a company's favor. That's true because when it comes to changing an organization, there are actually two processes at work, not just one. A medical analogy will help make this clear.

Consider what happens during a heart transplant. The first thing the doctor is concentrating on is the successful installation of the organ itself. He wants to make sure that it will function effectively with the rest of the body. The second thing the doctor must worry about is the body's rejection process. How is he going to deal with the antibodies that try to get any foreign body out of the system?

This rejection process is perfectly natural and rational. It is there for a purpose. When our forebears had a spear stuck in them, their bodies tried to get that foreign object out—and fast.

So, when going about performing the heart transplant, the doctor needs a separate set of procedures to manage these antibodies that he or she knows are going to pop up. Otherwise, the patient will be jeopardized.

An organization has "antibodies," too. And they perform exactly the same task as they do in the human body, protecting against an invasion of foreign objects, in this case foreign ideas. Again, this is an entirely rational process. A successful company does things in a certain way. Anything that threatens to attack the way it functions is to be rejected.

The problem, of course, is that just because a way of doing business was successful in the past doesn't mean that it will be successful in the future. Corporations do need to evolve. Yet that puts them smack up against the antibodies. Most change programs fail not because they aren't good ideas, but because the antibodies eventually get them.

The biggest mistake leaders make is assuming if they lead, people will follow. People are pretty smart. They will say, "Yes, boss, we will follow you, and your new change program, to the ends of the earth," and then they don't. Since they'll be punished for being openly disloyal, no one will openly say that they are not going to follow. They just don't tag along.

Their reaction is perfectly natural. They are comfortable doing things one way, so why would they willingly try to do it another? And why should they change just because the boss is giving them a new sales pitch? People are trying to sell them things every day. They are naturally skeptical.

You can't ignore this natural phenomenon. You have to accept the fact that antibodies are there and then figure out a way to get it to work in your favor. Given the history at WCIA, we had a daunting task ahead.

EMBRACING THE TIGER

The wonderful thing about WCIA was the ability of Jeff's management team to embrace the skepticism and work to turn it around. This takes guts. (It is also a subject that is rarely addressed in business schools.) It's far easier to ignore the skeptics or order them to obey. But his team is smarter than that.

Jeff himself, every stocky inch of him, was like a bulldog that would not let go of the change process no matter what happened. If you have ever had to stare down a bulldog on a dark street, you know that whoever blinks first is history. Jeff didn't blink. His team stood unflinchingly with him. They understood that not only would they have to acknowledge the skepticism that was running rampant through his company, but that they would also have to figure out a way to use that skepticism to their advantage. That would be a thought they would bring up again and again to us as they went about changing the company.

Most of our work was accomplished in workshop settings with anywhere from a dozen to three hundred people in attendance. Throughout the process, we were fortunate to work closely with Meg Johnston, the vice president of human resources, and her team, whose stamina and unrelenting attention to the whole process was essential to achieving success.

We decided we would start at the top of the organization, not because of the hierarchy, but because people won't change if they know that leadership is not truly committed. People spend an awful lot of time watching what the boss does. Even the slightest hint, through tone of voice or body language, that the boss is not truly committed to the idea being pushed will stop a new idea cold.

Conversely, change cannot come only from the top down. If it does, it will hit bedrock sooner or later. You need to have the people in the lower ranks of the organization buy in from the beginning as well.

With that in mind, we designed a change program that would follow this sequence:

1. We would start the senior management team rethinking where they wanted to take the business. The senior management team—dubbed the Strategy Group—initially would have fourteen members, although it grew to thirty-two over time.
2. The next couple of layers of management, about one hundred and fifty in all, participated in a meeting in New York to build their commitment to the draft vision and to the ongoing change process.
3. From there we would move to functional departments (marketing, finance, administration, etc.) and district offices from around the country.

4. Following that there would be large-scale meetings of several hundred people each who would gather in Fort Myers, Florida, to identify initiatives they could take to push this change forward.
5. Finally, we would help to introduce some of the skills necessary to turn the change process into a reality.

WCIA has just over two thousand people in North and South America. We would talk with each one of them—either individually or in small groups—over the next eighteen months.

The senior management team started meeting in November. The first order of business was to "embrace the tiger"—that is, to figure out how they were going to deal with the antibodies. We began discussing the problem in a workshop. That session began with us telling Jeff and his team what we had learned from our numerous interviews with WCIA's employees.

After hearing all the skepticism that those people had expressed—and we made sure we quoted them exactly—Jeff and his team might easily have packed it in right there. They were listening to their subordinates question management's commitment to quality and the breakdown of the corporate culture as well as state problems they had dealing with as a company run by people on the other side of the Atlantic.

While it would have been surprising if all of this had come as a shock—this had all been discussed in the corridors of WCIA's headquarters—it certainly was damning to listen to the unrelenting criticism of WCIA's employees. For those of us presenting the material, it was much like pointing a loaded shotgun in the face of a potential robbery victim.

We were concerned. One complicating factor at the early stage of the change process is the natural resistance of people inside an organization to accept strangers into the family, especially when the strangers (us) knew so much of the dirty laundry as they walked in the door. And not only did we know the dirty laundry, we were putting it right on the table for all to see.

As we learned from working with other companies, the only way management is going to accept outsiders is to have them come independently to the conclusion that they have no choice. They must reach the point of the alcoholic who awakens one morning after having slept in a ditch and then says, "That does it. I have to change." Unless management reaches that point, things don't really change. They have to say, "We have tried everything else, and we can't get there by trying harder. We are already working nights and weekends. We have to do something different."

There are occasionally times where this first jarring meeting is as far as we get. Management listens (seemingly) intently and then says something like, "Yes, but you are overstudying the problem," or "Yes, but there are positive things you are overlooking," or "Yes, but corporate won't let us." In those situations we know that management doesn't have the stomach for real change.

But to WCIA's credit, this was not one of those times. Everybody in the room realized that WCIA should—and indeed must—actively embrace the change process.

GETTING THE BALL ROLLING

We met with the senior management team every four to six weeks through the spring. What's more important is the process that the managers went through. In a traditional consulting approach, we would have first interviewed everyone at the company, then tried to figure out what was going on, and finally given a full report to the senior management team.

We don't work that way.

We think the key to implementing a change program is making the people in charge of change figure out what needs to be changed. Forcing them to do the work results in their truly understanding the issues plaguing the company. Even better, it compels everyone to think strategically.

This is important because the key people in the organization will become the missionaries for the change process. They will develop from students to teachers. The only way they will be able to do that is by truly understanding how their company operates, what works well and what needs changing. They will never gain that understanding by merely listening to some consultant present a report. They need to come out of this with "their answer," not ours. They had to "own" it. We could help, by acting as facilitators and providing information about how people in other industries were handling similar problems, but the ultimate decisions would have to be theirs.

Over the first six months, WCIA's senior management carved out a strong vision statement (to be discussed in a moment) that everyone in the company could get excited about. It focused on who WCIA's customer was and how the company was going to get a jump on its competitors. They also followed through with strategies to support this new vision.

KNITTING THE VISIONS TOGETHER

Once we had an organization-wide vision, it was taken out to the various functions and sales districts around the country. In working on its local vision, each department had to think about who the customer was. With the exception of sales and service, almost no one at WCIA had ever done that. In fact, they had never really seen a customer, nor thought they should have been concerned about having one.

Developing a clear understanding about who their customer was and determining how WCIA was to achieve its competitive advantage were the focus of many of our sessions.

And a funny thing happened at those sessions once we had representatives from different departments present. Members from the various departments started talking to one another and began developing common ground. Traditionally, people deal only with employees in their own departments, and as a result they become insular, developing their own terminology. When they meet with other departments for the first time, it is like listening to a Tower of Babel.

But here, in small groups, they started to work together. Everyone began trying to imagine who the customer was, and that established a common link. We were supposed to help solidify that link by getting them to discuss, and eventually accept, the vision Jeff and his team had crafted together.

It didn't work out that way.

BUILDING BUY-IN

Most organizations stop the change process after the senior management team has gotten its act together. Implementation usually consists of top-down communications and directives, often accompanied with a reorganization—just to keep people on their toes. The rationale behind a change process conducted this way is simple: People can be ordered to change their ways.

Needless to say, corporations that follow this approach have a track record for change that deserves a C− at best. Otherwise, our leading corporations wouldn't be in the mess they are in.

The reason for "change" being a tall order is that most of the effort is spent by senior management alone, insulated from the troops below. The top brass go off to fancy resorts in the mountains, hoping that the fresh air will stimulate their creativity. Harvard professors are invited to give them a peek at what's new in management, and the executives plan field trips to visit other leading corporations to learn the formula, with the hope that some of that success will rub off on them.

This kind of high-level "learning" is great because it opens up a whole new world. It shows the possibilities to the people driving the business. Unfortunately, while the top team gets weeks or months to wrestle with the new ideas and a prolonged period to adjust to the changes, the next layer down might have a one- or two-day "rollout meeting." And even less time is spent with employees further down the organization.

This kind of change process ends up with the poor guy on the shop floor watching a one-hour video of the company president extolling the importance of change. Then we wonder why he hasn't bought in. This approach to corporate change is so common that we have reduced it to a theorem that we call the Fizzle Principle. The principle? The amount of effort and resources spent in creating change is proportional to the individual's or group's level in the organization. The lower you are, the less you get.

From the beginning we had impressed on WCIA's management the fact that they would be better off not starting the change process than going this route. Real buy-in to organizational changes must involve each and every person rethinking his or her job, and deciding how he or she is going to reinvent their own work, in order to support the overall corporate vision. This is a tall order.

Many years ago, a relatively minor incident taught us a valuable lesson about "change." We were having lunch at a restaurant and the woman serving us was a charter airline flight attendant who waitressed when she was off duty to earn a little extra cash. Between the soup and the sandwich, she gave us what traditional consulting firms would have called the complete vision and competitive positioning of her airline and told how it affected her own job.

"We're in the cattle-car segment of the industry," she told us. "My customer is a person who likes to get a deal on the ticket. He's the kind of person who brags about how he got a $700 ticket for just $250 by waiting until the very last minute, when the airlines were desperate to unload seats on a charter flight. This is the kind of person who will tell anyone who asks, and often even people who don't, what a smart shopper he is.

"Given that these people believe that they are getting an absolute steal, my job is to make it extremely difficult to get a second cup of coffee. If I fall all over them with service, they'll think they paid too much for the ticket!"

She turned to pick up the check at a neighboring table but continued her story where she had left off when she returned a moment later.

"Our major competitor is in the 'vacation experience' market. Their customer is a two-career family who has decided that they have to get away. Planning the trip wasn't easy, they never could seem to be able to get their schedules to mesh, and getting to the airport wasn't any easier. The baby-sitter was late, and they have just managed to stem all the last-minute crises at their offices. They arrive running down the jetway to get on the plane, just before we shut the doors," our flight attendant/waitress continued.

"If I were working for that company, I would greet that couple in a hula skirt and hand them a rum swizzle, complete with one of those little umbrellas in it, and stereo headphones the moment they walked on the plane so they would know they were *on vacation*. I would pamper them so much that they would remember the airplane trip as much as the time at their destination."

She had completely internalized her company's strategy (and her competitor's while she was at it) and reinvented her job to support it.

This is how real change comes about, as each person—at every level of the organization—rethinks his or her role. In contrast, the traditional notion says that change evolves out of a strategy that is carved out at the top of the organization and then is "implemented" or "rolled out" below. That rarely works well because the people down below don't know where and how they are supposed to fit in. More important, they rarely have the chance to think through how their job, and life, has changed as a result of the shake-up in the company.

The overall objective of our change process was to have each person or group rethink their role just as the flight attendant/waitress did.

In May, we started working with WCIA's various departments such as marketing, finance, accounting, operations (the computer systems people) as well as with about half a dozen sales districts across North and South America to help them do just that. We worked closely with Meg Johnston and her team.

THE VISION THAT DIDN'T FLY

It was supposed to be a rousing success. The senior management team had labored long and hard to create a vision statement. Tonight, the 150 managers from around the country who had gathered at New York were supposed to examine it, perhaps tweak it a bit, and then give it a rousing endorsement.

It didn't happen that way, although things began just as we had planned. The newly hatched vision was presented to a hushed crowd.

> WCI America will be the leader in providing products that integrate computer and information environments.
>
> Speed and usability will be our watchwords, and we will be responsive and innovative in satisfying customers.
>
> In doing this, we will ensure that we meet our goals of long-term growth and increasing profitability.
>
> The principles of fairness, integrity and respect for others will underlie all our activities. We will develop a diverse organization that thrives on teamwork, initiative and continuous improvement of our skills.

Instead of trying to "sell" the vision or to defend it, the management had the whole group break out into half a dozen large teams to work through people's suggestions for the vision statement. Each word of the original vision, along with every proposed change, came under intense scrutiny. Then the attacks began.

"Motherhood," said one person. "How can anyone want to be against being a leader?"

"Too wordy," said another. "This is suppose to inspire us? It would take a forklift just to pick the thing up."

"You don't believe this," said a third. "Management won't follow through and do whatever it takes to turn the vision into reality. It will be just like the quality program all over again."

In retrospect, you might say the managers were just releasing their frustrations that had been building since the quality program began. You could look for other explanations. The hour was too late, the people were too tired, and the unresolved issues that needed to be settled before drafting a vision statement were too large in scope to be knocked off in such an unwieldy meeting.

What emerged from the intense conversations was that WCIA should become the "innovator" (it was currently a sluggish follower) and be the "best" (i.e., number one) in integrating the world of their clients. (This instead of being the best at any one part of the total system, as a niche player would do.) This was a clear strategic choice about what WCIA should be, rather than mere word-smithing.

While lots of new thoughts were added, and debated, there was strong pressure to keep the statement short—and it was. By any measure the revised vision statement below represents a vast improvement. Far more important, the people had reinvented the vision and it was theirs—they owned it. They all cheered!

> WCI America is committed to meeting the needs of our clients with highly responsive service and innovative products. We will be the leader in integrating the complex information and computing needs that drive our customers' competitive advantage.

THE "PANEL OF DEATH"

It was late in the evening as the cheers for the new vision had barely died down. We should have stopped there while we were ahead. But there was one more event on the agenda —an open session to identify what was impeding progress. The senior management sat huddled together on a platform in front of everybody. When a particular issue was put forward by the audience, one of them was supposed to stand up and take ownership to "fix it," promising when he or she would report back on how the issue was to be resolved.

Unfortunately, people were tired and the group was too big to make this kind of thing work. The barrage came without stopping. "We are too slow in getting new products out the door" was the first issue. "When will head-count reductions stop?" was another. The attacks continued almost endlessly as top management sat behind the long table in the front of everyone and were verbally pilloried. At first, the bravest of them tried to field answers. Then the whole thing collapsed and we had to blow the whistle.

A small group of us, including the senior management, huddled together after what was instantly dubbed the Panel of Death to decide what to do. The only good thing was that it was the end of the day and we had overnight to try to think of something. Unfortunately, no matter how you tried to rationalize it, two things remained clear. First, the presentation was a disaster, and second, there was no way to paper over it.

Undoubtedly somewhere there is some Chinese philosopher, perhaps Confucius, who said that in all adversity is opportunity. Eventually we realized that this disaster—and there was no other word that could adequately describe it—gave the team the opportunity to demonstrate that employees could make mistakes and not be shot for it.

Where better to start than with the president. The next morning, the mood was electric as Jeff addressed the crowd. Everybody wondered what he would say.

"Last night," he began, "we tried something in good faith—a process to involve all of you in wrestling with the issues we all must face. Unfortunately," he continued, "we blew it. It simply bombed."

A round of applause went up, probably a sign of relief from the tension in the crowd. "As we move through change, however, we all will make mistakes, because change is about taking risks, and risks means there will be more mistakes. We can't just roll over when something goes wrong, we must bounce back. We must learn from what has happened, and forge ahead."

As the morning continued, the mood of skepticism shifted to one of buoyant enthusiasm. The president had shown himself as human and had the stature and grace to face his mistake head-on.

"Walk the talk" is an all-too-common phrase in management today, but few ever really model the behavior they are espousing. In the days of trench warfare, the commander was always the first over the hill into the blazing guns. Today, he is usually safely back at headquarters preparing an alibi, in case something goes wrong.

Here, Jeff and his team had demonstrated true leadership and had paved the way for his people. Nothing builds credibility more than leading by doing.

THE REINVENTION OF THE PRESIDENT

On the final day, Jeff got up to give the closing address. Gone were the TelePrompTers, the endlessly rehearsed addresses and the carefully couched corporate language. He marched right out onto center stage, leaving the lectern behind.

In the hushed room, he told passionately of his own personal odyssey and experience with change, starting in Liverpool as a child of a single parent. People had not seen this side of him. He was human, with hopes and fears just like them. Could this really be the same tough finance guy who always talked in terms of numbers and head-count reductions? Here was a leader being born, rising to the occasion. Any doubts about his commitment vanished, and for the first time, people wanted to follow. The crowd had never seen anything like it and went wild. They hooted, they yelled, they stomped their feet.

THE CHANGE CONTINUES

The journey is far from over for WCIA, but these initial exciting events sent a strong signal to people that the times were really changing. The leadership of the business learned to change the way they themselves worked, setting an example for others.

It isn't surprising, then, to note that in the year following that final meeting, the company profits turned round. They went from a $9 million loss to a $15 million profit; a $50 million profit was forecast for the following year. Can this all be attributed to the program? No, not all. The improving market certainly helped. However, the greater responsiveness and teamwork enabled WCIA to seize these opportunities. Products are being introduced faster, and WCIA is beginning to overtake its niche competitors. The change has taken root.

STAGE 2 GOLDEN RULES

- **The customer, a flag outside**

There are no shortcuts! WCIA made the effort to provide everybody in the organization with a structured opportunity to think about the customer and to reinvent their work to add value to the customer. The focus outside allowed the organization to unlock ongoing disputes that had been going on for years.

- **Teams need leaders**

Talking is at the heart of team formation. When people discuss the business in a structured way, they start moving away from the "we/they" situation, where the blame is always somewhere else. They learn to take the initiative to improve things rather than wait for someone else. However, the euphoria from the sense of empowerment has to be balanced by "accountability" for hard results—this is management's role. Leaders cannot abrogate their responsibility to lead—the free rein must be matched by a willingness to intervene when things get off track.

• Learning to play together

Cooperative behavior doesn't happen automatically, it has to be built in. And the best place to start is during the Strategic Planning Process. Thinking strategically about the business at all levels is an ongoing process which needs to be built in just as you would any other management control system. That process must not be allowed to become a sterile number-crunching exercise. Make it a process of involvement and you get cooperation as a matter of course.

The Guerrilla

Buried in many large bureaucracies are hothouses of innovation where bright, dedicated people toil away, largely unnoticed by the larger system. At best they are tolerated; at worst they are branded as corporate mavericks and lose their power, likely victims of the next round of cost cutting.

Jack Kirkbride was a brave innovator, an innovator being suffocated by the bureaucracy. He did the only thing he could under the circumstances; like a guerrilla, he kept his head below the vegetation so he wouldn't be shot.

Jack's war was a lonely one. He fought it with conviction. To the surprise of almost everybody within the organization, he won. With little fanfare, he dismantled the formal management structure within his company and replaced it with highly entrepreneurial, self-managing teams.

Jack started at Stage 2 of the shift to the Molecular Organization, trying to get teamwork and cooperation going in a very hostile environment. He wrestled with some formidable obstacles—the internal management system and the expectations of the very people he was seeking to empower.

You are about to learn how the loyal organization man became a guerrilla fighter.

"It was Dave Stuart who really got me started," Jack Kirkbride recalled as he sat down with us over lunch. "He had this thing about teamwork which he got me to believe in. Our enthusiasm led us a little astray, but our hearts were always in the right place, and in the end, we truly did change this company."

Kirkbride, a quiet, contemplative engineer, was the head of development for one of the country's largest engineering companies. He knew that the typical pyramid organizational structure he was working in was slowing up the development of new products. Even worse, he knew that it was sapping the creative talents of the people who worked for him. They were spending too much time fighting turf wars with other engineering groups within the company and not enough time creating new products.

Something had to change. In common with most change

agents, Jack had a buddy. Change is a lonely process and you can use all the support you can get. Dave was a refugee from marketing who had found his way into the development department. His job to bring the products Jack's people developed out of engineering and into the marketplace. Cheerful and ebullient, Dave was Jack's probe into the organization. He was a kind of walking thermometer, measuring morale in real time, and Jack tended to rely heavily on his advice. They spent long evenings after work talking about how bureaucratic engineering was becoming and what they could do about it.

"I had a very clear understanding of the problem," Jack recalls. "We were developing products at half the speed of our competitors, and at a much higher cost, and the biggest cost was people.

"I knew we had to take costs out, but I was stymied. At the time, it was almost impossible to find your way through all the barriers the company had set up to cut costs—particularly people costs." Jack's solution was to change the way people worked. He would make them more efficient. He'd free up man-hours and then scour the company for more work to keep his developers busy.

"The real answer was to get rid of the 25 percent of my staff that was unproductive. Company procedures made that impossible. And I guess I went along with the prevailing wisdom that people could be trained to do just about anything," Jack added. "The people who I really should have let go—the paper shufflers and managers who had fallen behind technically—would be wondrously transformed into developers by the application of a liberal dose of training. I knew things didn't usually happen like this in real life, but I was convinced that I had found the solution to all my woes."

But how exactly would all these people work differently? Jack wasn't sure, and so he asked Dave.

"Teamwork," Dave replied, as if the answer was obvious.

Development projects at the time were done in small work teams. As a result, there were big gaps between the people and groups who were working on different parts of the same project. Delays were caused by both duplication of effort and lack of commitment. People reinvented ideas that they didn't know had been created. Worse, they got attached to their particular version of the answer. This led to endless battles over ideas. As a result, Jack was spending an unacceptable chunk of his time trying to satisfy warring factions.

All of this chewed up development time, dollars and emotional energy. Worse, it made engineering look inward. More time was being spent on internal fights than on trying to satisfy the customer.

Dave's idea was simple. If they could get all the developers to see themselves as part of a whole, part of a team, then he figured a lot of the problems of poor communication and internal bickering would go away.

Jack, who has had the benefit of twenty-twenty hindsight, gave us his evaluation of those early efforts in establishing teams.

"We didn't go in for what we would now call 'in-depth teamwork training,' " he explains. "Looking back, I'd say we gravitated to more of a motivational approach. We were pretty naive in those days."

Jack took his people on team-building experiences. They went on Outward Bound trips, and they hired motivational speakers who inflated people's spirits. They held seminars, roundtable discussions about the problems of cooperation, and talked constantly about how everyone should seek to work more in the interests of the company as a whole.

The results were like an adrenaline shot. Everyone got pumped up for a few hours or even a few days. Then cooperation slowed because things were just too difficult and stopped.

"The program was going nowhere, so, of course, our

reaction was to do a more intense version of more of the same," Jack says. "We developed another, more comprehensive program of more rah-rah stuff that all managers and all members of the professional staff had to attend."

"This went on for two years. The adrenaline spikes got higher and higher. But when they wore off, people got even more depressed about how things were going," Jack added. "Everybody was starting to get fed up.

"We had succeeded in raising awareness about the issue of failing to work as a team," he added. "But we had given no real guidance on how to work as a team. We were all encouragement and no content. The developers gave us an A for effort, and an A+ for sincerity, but a failing grade for getting anything actually done."

Even worse, by rubbing everyone's nose in the problem, and then failing to deliver a plan for making things better, Jack was creating resistance. Repeated failure to impact behavior on a sustained basis was leading to cynicism and finger pointing. At first the complaints were voiced against other colleagues and teams, but gradually people started to generalize the issues to the company as a whole and began to see themselves as victims of a "system" failure.

And they had a point. The most glaring examples of poor teamwork were in the company's top management. The poorest communications and most constricted channels were between the managers of the company's various operations.

"I came to realize that a lot of what the people were complaining about was right," Jack says. "It was about then that I really began to understand the fact that I was trying to create a major cultural shift, and I was trying to do it against the backdrop of the company's management system, a system that saw no reason to change. Just about everyone thought things were running smoothly."

The best example was measurement.

WHAT GETS MEASURED GETS DONE?

"Look, everyone in the company is basically an engineer," Jack explains. "The company was measurement ob-
sessed then, and it is to this day. Everyone has the basic
engineering mentality: If it can't be measured, it isn't real.
You can't control it, so why do you want to talk about it?

"But our company put a particular twist on measurement when it came to measuring performance," he added.
"The company operated on a system of 'management by
objectives.' Under this idea, each individual had clearly defined tasks for which he or she was responsible and would be
rewarded or punished for how well he or she performed
them.

"However, over the years, the system had been refined to
an almost jewel-like beauty. Performance reviews were indeed tied to objectives. Rewards were calculated to the second decimal place. Everyone was reviewed with an almost
religious observance of ritual, but the system had become a
liability. People had stopped worrying about what was the
right thing to do, and spent their time worried about what
their performance contract said that they had to do," Jack
recalled.

"In a fast-moving world, such rigidity was crazy. Worse,
people clung to their responsibilities like leeches, preventing
others from making changes. They were carving out turf
where none should have existed, and then they fought to
protect every last blade of grass. The system told them who
they were, and what they did, and so they weren't going to
do a thing to jeopardize it.

"But all those measures we had put in place over the
years didn't do a damn thing for us except slow us down, for
one overriding reason," Jack continued. "Achieving anything required team cooperation. After all, I can't be success-

ful unless you have done your bit and I've done mine. But with the measures focusing on individuals and no individual able to control his environment, everybody's personal strategy was reduced to proving that whatever failures took place weren't their fault. They had done their job.

"We spent too much time evaluating excuses, excuses that really implied that somebody else had fouled up."

Since everyone is bound to fail on something, there was an unspoken consensus within the company that no one could be blamed for anything. The result was that bonuses were never significant, but no one ever suffered a reduction in income for failure either.

"But you couldn't say any of that publicly," Jack is quick to point out. "The system demanded that the performance ritual be danced, even if it drove people apart."

That was bad, of course, but the situation was actually far worse.

"We really depended on other parts of engineering to do things for us," Jack explains. "But cooperation was almost impossible. Everyone reported to somewhere else within the firm, and so it was almost impossible to have accountability. You'd expect something to be delivered, and it wouldn't appear. When you tried to find out what had gone wrong, you'd find that someone had yanked someone's chain in another location, and as a result, your project had been downgraded in importance, and the only way to get it back on line was to go to war.

"It got so bad that we hated doing business with other parts of engineering. If we had a choice, we would always work with an outside supplier. They were motivated to serve us, and at least in dealing with them, we could control our own destiny. We were not alone in this. Everyone thought this way.

"But the twist lies in the failure of the others to deliver, which meant that everyone had a built-in excuse to fail. You could always blame your failure to perform on someone else not supplying you with what you needed."

The result was that any camaraderie and teamwork in Jack's operation was about panning the internal company "opposition" and not about making the business hum or drawing together to take care of a customer. And teamwork training hadn't made the situation better. It had actually made things worse.

"And yet my gut told me that we were on the right track," Jack says. "Our initial analysis of the situation had been spot on. We had to find a way of pulling this operation together as a business and making it work as a single unit. Our take was that teamwork was the way to do it. Our technique was not working, but we were still convinced that teamwork was the way to go."

Part of Jack's problem was the concept he and Dave had of what makes a team. Dave had formed his vision out of his marketing background. His model was an account team serving a customer. In advertising, the account rep has a very clear focus—the customer—and an equally clear incentive to make that customer happy: income. The more ads a client runs, the more money the agency makes.

The problem was that neither of these conditions existed in engineering. Products were created for the company, but it could be for any part of the company, so there was no clear focus on an internal customer. And since these products were often combined with the outputs of other locations, it was difficult to focus on the end user.

In terms of compensation, as we have seen, there was no clear connection between effort and reward.

"As we mulled all this over, what really seemed to stick out was a lack of focus," Jack said. "The lack of pulling together for a common purpose. We had just about reached this conclusion when we met you guys."

ESPRIT DE CORPS

Again, it was Dave, as Jack's scout, who had been the catalyst. He had heard us speak at a local seminar and liked what he heard us say about dispersed organizational structures, values and teamwork. The idea of a Molecular Organization had struck a particularly responsive cord with him.

He contacted us and the four of us met over lunch to talk about the issues plaguing engineering.

"At that first meeting I became a convert," Jack told us later. "What you guys were saying seemed to explain what I was going through, but could never put into words. Most of all, you gave me a sense of being in the flow of history, that what I was going through, what the company was going through, was inevitable. Since it was inevitable, I saw my job as going with the flow and guiding the change that was bound to take place."

This sense of destiny was crucial. Jack was already beginning to see that achieving real change was a time-consuming process. His estimate, which jibes with the experience of people who had been in similar situations, was that trying to change engineering was taking between 50 percent and 70 percent of his time at work. And yet as far as the company was concerned, what he was doing was an indulgence, something to be carried on in his spare time once his normal management load was complete. Company executives really didn't see why engineering's organizational structure had to change, but if Jack wanted to fiddle with it, it was fine with them, as long as he got his work done.

As Jack put it: "The environment was passive. As long as I didn't threaten any of the cherished ideas put forth by the people in human resources, I was free to try to 'raise morale' as much as I liked."

Human resources and the issue of morale would be a continuing sore point through the next few years, as Jack began pushing ever more vigorously at the boundaries of what the people in personnel thought was acceptable. Morale was more than just a touchy-feely concept at the company. Like everything else it was measured. The yardstick was the morale survey.

The survey was one of the company's key measurements of managerial effectiveness. A manager's staff was polled annually and asked to give their opinion of their boss's performance and also asked how they felt in general about the company and what it was doing. A part of the company from the beginning, the survey had taken on a life of its own.

"The poll was very threatening to managers and was sometimes manipulated by employees," Jack explained. "Everyone would be on edge for weeks before and after the reading was taken. You were compared against other locations and with your prior scores, and by implication, although we could never prove it, with the scores of your peers."

Jack had never had a particularly bad survey, but he had seen the effects that a bad score had had on others. A poor morale survey was a major blot on your career; a great one was proof positive of your capability as a manager, and by implication on your promotability. Jack's approval rating had been in the 60 percent range for a number of years—safely above the norm for the company—and his efforts at teamwork improvement had pushed him up a few points. Ergo, his program, even though it really hadn't accomplished anything, was a success in the eyes of the company's management system.

The fact that he was trying to improve profits instead of morale was not factored into anyone's thinking. As morale had not declined, he had permission to continue.

This faulty logic just confirmed something Jack and Dave had known for years: Human resources, the guardian of the morale survey, was no longer the company's strong suit. Once a leader in its people practices, the company had let the department atrophy. Ideas such as the morale survey gave the company a probe into evaluating the organization, but the ideas had taken on a bureaucratic life of their own. The concepts of performance measurement, pay and employment practices had become sclerotic.

Yet H.R. still had enormous influence—in its ability to stop things. The process it had put in place for hiring and firing people had become so onerous that you just about had to steal the crown jewels to be fired, and would-be employees had to jump over numerous hurdles to get hired.

If Jack was going to make real change happen, he would run straight into H.R. Any slip in the morale survey would bring him under scrutiny. Yet if he was going to change things, he was going to have to bend some rules—including the sacrosanct ones that surrounded performance appraisal and how his people were paid. Any deviation from standard H.R. practices would be hard to explain.

"The threat of having to explain was very real," Jack recalled. "To an outsider, this can sound peculiar. But the company took its established policies very seriously. It wasn't so much the explanation itself that people feared. It was the terrible waste of time."

Having a belief in the "flow of history" was therefore critical to Jack. It gave him confidence that he was on the right track in his decision to try to change the organization. However, that was cold comfort when it came to day-to-day dealings at the company. He was subject to steady attacks about what he was trying to do. There was constant sniping about whether his ideas about teamwork matched the accepted practices at the company. Merely being right—and making engineering more efficient—would not be enough.

As a result of our lunch, we agreed to give a speech as part of another morale-building day at the lab. Jack introduced us and we stood up in front of the whole organization and told our story. Several hundred developers, mostly young, but with a sprinkling of gray hair here and there, heard us out in silence.

When Jack stood up to ask for questions, once we were done, the response he got was interesting. The audience was way ahead of him.

"I later discovered this was common," Jack recalls. "We would make a proposal, or bring forward an idea, and the reaction from our organization was 'What took you so long?' Unfortunately, this gave us a false sense of their willingness to change. They were intellectually there, but almost none of them had the remotest idea of what working in a new way implied in practice. As the implications began to sink in, and they realized that they themselves were the ones who had to change, resistance sprang up."

But at the moment, the overwhelming feeling was that change was, indeed, "in the flow of history." The people resonated to the ideas and reinforced all of Jack's previous efforts.

"What they told me after your speech was 'They're absolutely right, of course. We do have to reorganize the company. We've known that forever. What are you going to do about it?' "

Faced with this question, Jack did the only thing that made sense. He made a commitment then and there in front of the group to undertake a change process. He vowed to lead the charge into the new world.

We recommended that Jack begin his efforts at changing engineering by starting with his top management team. They would have to buy in first. If they didn't, they would poison the well, and the rest of his organization would not follow. People are not going to give a 100 percent commitment to a new program if they know their boss is against it.

After meeting with Jack and Dave, we suggested that he gather his top management and, in a series of meetings, hammer out a new strategy. We thought it was important for them to build the strategy together. This would give them insight into the business, build teamwork and perform a useful educative function. It would help them learn some of the tools that are needed to think strategically.

We ran a series of workshops addressing key strategic issues, starting with our basic question of "Who is the customer?" The first workshop went well, with the top fifteen managers attending. People tried and worked diligently on the questions we gave them about what their customers valued, and the like.

But from the first session it was a shaky process.

"The basic problem was that we were not a single business, had never been one and could not conceive of being one," Jack told us during a break. "They think that no matter how enlightening these exercises are, they are at their heart academic. They just don't think that they will ever be able to run their part of engineering like a business. Since that's true, they have an impossible time at seeing it as a business."

This wasn't for a lack of potential. The operation had all the earmarks of a business. It had customers. It sold its development services, and it was measured on various parameters of effectiveness. It would have been very easy for the top management team to see itself as a business, specifically to see itself as a contract development house.

But many of the managers just couldn't buy into the idea of being a business—and for good reason. They saw their work assignments as arbitrary. They knew that at any moment they could be closed down or expanded, all at the whim of "corporate." This lack of control over their own destiny was crippling. The response from just about everybody was to work hard, keep your nose clean and do your professional duty—and not one thing more.

This pervasive sense of not being a business haunted the

process. No matter what was done, it was always there. Not for everyone, but for enough of the participants that it muddied the principal objective of the change program, which is to create a sense of cohesion around the customer and the group's business objective.

"This was one of the most frustrating things I have ever been involved with," Jack says. "We were producing some wonderful ideas about how to be a business-oriented development organization. We were learning a tremendous amount about how the world was changing and how it was moving toward concepts such as mass customization. But I couldn't get people to change. They felt they had no control over their own destiny, and so they said to themselves, 'Why bother?' "

"The frustrating thing about their attitude was that it was at total odds with our history," Jack added. "We had never sat around waiting for work. We had a reputation as an aggressive entrepreneurial place. Yet no matter how hard I pushed them, they couldn't shake the feeling that nothing they did would matter, that they would always be at the whim of the people at corporate."

As the change program progressed, Jack stopped focusing on the group as a whole and honed in more on some of the key members. He thought if we educated them and turned them into a cadre around whom he could build the future, the rest of the group would come around to the new way of thinking.

To find out if his idea was working, Jack asked Dave to take the pulse of the participants. What he learned was that there was a lot of confusion, fear, aggression and uncertainty —the standard fare of a change in process. But instead of taking this anxiety as a sign that the change process was underway, Jack saw it as a threat to the process. He started to get worried, despite our reassurances.

"You guys told me not to worry. That this was normal.

That without resistance there would be no change. But my engineering training caught me. I wanted linear progress. I know now that isn't possible in behavioral change, but I didn't know it at the time."

In the midst of his concern, Jack repeatedly held meetings about "where we were in the change process." Those discussions always had an easy answer. In terms of schedule, you could say we are 37.3 percent of the way there, or whatever. But they were almost impossible to answer in terms of where behavioral change was at a given moment.

By the end of the summer of 1990, Jack was beginning to enter the darkest phase of his change journey which had begun two years before. They had made good progress. He had a detailed business plan for his operation, one that called for it to operate as a freestanding development house. That meant technically he could claim victory and justify the time and money spent trying to change the lab.

But he also had a management team that was polarized.

At one end of the spectrum, he had those who wanted to tear up the old structure and old ways and create new, flat, empowered, Molecular Organizations. At the other, he had those who were mired in hierarchical, top-down, "tell me what you want, and I'll do it" thinking.

Jack himself? He was in Fiji!

"I thought long and hard before I made that trip. My wife and I had planned it for years, but to take a month off at this point in the change process was tricky. I almost canceled it two or three times, but I'm glad we went through with it. Getting far away gave me the perspective I needed."

By the time Jack came back, he had come to some clear decisions.

"I realized that I had no choice but to keep going forward," he concluded. "I realized that I was not going to be able to take everyone with me at the same speed, and that was okay. I would concentrate on those who really wanted to change and then use them as examples for the rest. I was convinced that my initial decision to focus on a small group was correct.

"However, after thinking about the situation on the trip, I concluded that the chosen ones were going to have to be driven further and farther than I had ever thought of doing, and to accomplish that, I knew I was going to tear up the organization. What I wanted to create couldn't be done piecemeal, or placed on top of what had gone before. I was going to have to create a new organization."

Jack had discovered the basic rule of change: You can't change a system by playing with only one variable. Teamwork would be a foundation activity, but he was going to have to change other parts of the system to release the energy needed.

Human resources wasn't going to like it. They had to be squared away first.

"Dave and I had long conversations about how we were going to get H.R. on our side. The mere fact that we had to have those conversations was kind of bizarre, really. They were supposed to be on our side, but they weren't. They were more interested in making sure all the right forms were filled out than anything else. But all I needed was human resources to receive a complaint from someone that what we were doing was contrary to practice or that they felt discriminated against, and our lives would be misery."

They set about finding a sponsor as far up the organization ladder as possible. In a previous incarnation, Dave had worked for a person who was a bit of a maverick; this man was now occupying a senior human resources staff post in the head office. Dave's former boss had nothing to do directly with Jack's operation, but he was an "in," nevertheless. Dave made a phone call and hit gold, the protection they needed. They could run an experiment that would empower some of the people in the lab, but no one could lose their job as a result, and Jack wouldn't be able to expand the experiment to the rest of his group until a full evaluation had been done.

"All these restraints were really a load of horsefeathers," Jack says. "They were desperate to cover themselves. On the one hand, the system clearly wasn't working. On the other, they didn't dare change it. So they let me take the lead, and reserved the right to criticize and judge the outcome."

While the situation was far from perfect, at least Jack had a chance to take an officially sanctioned swing at the change process.

But just as he had gotten authorization, another problem popped up: The company decided to introduce a total quality management program. Fortunately for Jack, this problem presented him with an enormous opportunity.

A SECRET WEAPON?

"The way we implemented TQM was typical of what was wrong with the company," Jack recalls. "Luckily, I was able to avoid the first wave, and as a result, I could turn the company's mistake into an opportunity.

"My first introduction to TQM was at the local manager's quality kickoff session," he explains. "We were told about the new corporate intent to improve quality, given a binder of papers filled with ideas, and told we should be a hundred percent committed to quality improvements. The entire execution of the TQM program was awful."

The binder was well printed and comprehensive. It was a masterful piece of work. The managers were supposed to learn the material, train their subordinate managers and then leave them to work out the details about how it should be implemented in their departments.

Jack was appalled. The stuff seemed complicated. It focused on manufacturing, not engineering, and he just knew that it was going to be rejected by his managers and professional staff. When you are asking people to change behavior, if the examples you give them are not addressed to them exactly, they find these examples hard to follow, and even harder to accept.

And then it got worse. Not surprisingly, a decision was made to measure the effectiveness of TQM.

The worldwide head of engineering created a set of overall measures of quality. Every single person was to contribute to improving those overarching measures and would be measured on the local level as well.

"I am not against measuring quality improvements," Jack is quick to say. "The problem was this program was all about product defects, and not in the least about whether the customer cared even remotely about the products we were improving. Our customer research told us categorically that they expected a few defects in leading-edge products. They were much more interested in how up-to-date the product was. They were prepared to trade off a few minor defects, as long as we promptly fixed them, which we always had in the past."

Jack moved as slowly as he could in implementing the TQM program into his operation. But even the early mentions of it set his organization into an uproar. The complaints were vocal and accurate:

- **Measurement-itis had just been given a new twist.**
- **Hours every month are going to have to be devoted to preparing presentations on the improvements that had or had not been achieved in quality.**
- **More time wasted.**
- **More lost weekends spent on retreats.**
- **More meaningless meetings.**

It was clear that the TQM program was going to cause serious problems for Jack's department.

"The more I looked at the program, the less I liked it," he said. "It was one of a long line of such programs that had washed over us in the past. I was sure it would pass eventually —this sort of program always disappears without a trace in time—but in the interim it could very destructive to our development effectiveness.

"First, there was no connection to the strategy of the business," Jack says. "My experience in trying to develop a strategy earlier in the year had sensitized me to the need to make everything emanate from a singular point of view, the point of view of the customer in our case.

"The program we were provided with simply didn't do that. We were asked to learn the vocabulary of quality, which is not exactly complicated, and then apply it to reducing defects. But the materials we were given provided us with no means of discussing where the customer fit in with all this.

"Second, there was no effective mechanism for helping people absorb this mass of material," Jack says. "The program was to be rolled out in the traditional way. Just like all those other programs that hadn't made it. We were trapped as a company in an old way of thinking. We had tried all the new management ideas as they emerged during the 1970s and 1980s. We had even tried some, like quality, in several different incarnations. They all made a little bit of a difference. But none of them really changed us. We just kept overlaying them on the old ways we did business and nothing really changed. "The people were pretty sick of it all," he continues. "And rightfully so."

The major problem, as Jack saw it, was that the employees weren't given enough time to accept the new program and adjust to it.

"When they were looking at the program, the top management team went for three days to several companies with strong quality programs. That was a heck of a commitment. They bought into the idea, worked on its adaptation, then handed it over to the people in the trenches to train the managers on the principles.

"Well, we've got a standard approach for that," Jack continues. "We use classic classroom teaching methods: presentations and question-and-answer sessions. We would even include room at the end for personal agenda setting and commitments. We knew that the material was inevitably complex and that time was short. But these are smart people and they mostly understood it at an intellectual level.

"Managers were then expected to go away, work out quantitative measures—'People do what you measure' is our corporate motto, you know—and get on with things. For the large majority of incremental improvements in a stable hierarchical organization, this process works. In holistic change situations it is not effective, because you are not touching behavior."

A huge reason for that was the inability to tailor the canned classroom TQM experience to the needs of the people in Jack's operation. The way it was set up, one size was supposed to fit all, and Jack knew from experience that just wouldn't work.

"You've got to appreciate the depth of cynicism that greeted these classroom-based behavior-change programs," Jack explained. "People went into the room where the TQM program was being presented and they were promptly turned off. The one-way communication did not even penetrate their minds. We needed something that would engage them and show them how the material could help them do their jobs better."

Intriguingly, the failure gave Jack, and us, an opportunity. Eventually even the designers of the program realized that it was flawed.

Jack went to them with a daring idea.

"Look," he said, "my morale survey scores show that my change idea had some promise. Why don't you let me see if I can help with TQM?"

Jack's idea was simple: He would bring us in to present the TQM program. While we were at it, we agreed to also spread the word about the change process, a detail we conveniently forgot to mention to the H.R. department. The principal constraint was that we had to use the provided TQM materials as the core of our program. So we set out to wrap the change program in a strategic envelope, making sure that all the while we would be stressing the virtues of TQM, but starting with the customer.

Our approach of starting with the customer solved Jack's fundamental problem with the company's quality program, which was not based on anything that the customer wanted. We stressed that all the quality improvements in the world wouldn't mean a thing if the customer didn't care about what you were improving.

An understanding of the customer and what he or she valued gave obvious insight into the defects issue. There are hundreds of processes that can be improved in a complex organization, but only a handful are a real priority. Entering a quality program without rooting it in what the customer wants means that there is no guidance about which processes are a priority and which are unimportant.

The solution to this turns out to be easy. The critical factors that will allow you to serve the customer successfully each contain implied processes. Those are the priority processes. For example, in engineering, the key is to develop a continuous stream of new ideas. That means communication between the developers was a top priority, as was continuous communication between the sales department and engineering, to guarantee Jack's people were staying on top of what the customer wanted. Improving those things would take precedence over making sure the company was using the most up-to-date order sheets, or making sure expense accounts were filled in exactly, to use easy examples.

"It had never occurred to us to look at processes this way," Jack said. "But when you do, it becomes obvious. You now know which processes are key. The idea that the judge of the effectiveness of a process lies outside the organization, with the customer, was a major insight. We now knew why we were improving a process, and what it had to yield."

Once these ideas were embedded, training people in ideas like process improvement techniques, defect elimination methods, measurement tools and the rest of the paraphernalia of quality became dramatically easier. Once they had the context, the ideas made sense.

Getting at the "rollout" problem also turned out to be fairly easy. We recommended that the TQM program we were doing be run in the same format for all levels in the organization, giving everyone an equal opportunity to learn it. Further, we suggested that people attend the sessions with their work teams so that they could take back with them the ideas they had learned with their group.

Traditionally, they would have attended based on time and availability and would have gone back to their jobs, excited by the new ideas they had heard, only to meet skeptical colleagues, who had not yet gone through the training. Much of the benefit would have been lost that way.

Finally, we designed a program that used their day-to-day experiences to illustrate the quality issue. We made them work through an example of a key process while they were still attending the training session, and we made them do it as a team. By the time they left, they each had had a chance to do a hands-on piece of work on a quality issue that affected their department every day.

All of this enhanced the program. That in and of itself was revolutionary.

"We had people from the quality department attending the sessions, auditing what we were doing," Jack recalls. "Eventually, even they had to admit that our approach was way ahead of what the rest of the organization was doing."

But these improvements paled beside the other opportunity that TQM presented Jack with.

Tacked on the back of the "official" curriculum that we had been given to work with was a token bow in the direction of empowerment. We say token because the material provided was sparse and weak. But for a man looking for a hook on which to hang his next attack on teamwork, the sparseness was a blessing. It meant that Jack could do his own thing.

"For the first time an official company program had given me the excuse I needed to talk about teamwork and participation," Jack recalled. "The new buzzword was empowerment, but it was really what I had been trying to get at all along."

With the TQM program underway, and the opportunities it offered for structured discussion officially sanctioned, Jack now could try to change his department into a different kind of organization. He decided to go Molecular.

A FRONTAL ASSAULT

Jack was an entrepreneur at heart. He had been scouring the company for new work for some time. And in the fall of 1990 he found it: a major program that would initially require eighty developers, but would rapidly rise to over two hundred, about a quarter of the people who worked for him.

The program was to last three years, in its initial phases, and success could stretch it out further. This was a high-profile opportunity, and Jack decided to use it as a chance to change his culture. To run this project he designed and implemented what he called a "circles" organization because of the way a Molecular Organization looks when drawn.

"This really broke the mold. Not only did we draw the organization differently, we rid it of some long-standing traditions, traditions that were making it harder for us to do anything."

Under the traditional way of doing things, Jack's initial group of eighty developers would have had eleven managers responsible for the efficient development of new products. The long-standing distinction between the managers and the developers—known internally as professionals—was profound. Managers were part of the official hierarchy of the business. They were higher up the chain of command and made administrative and strategic decisions. Professionals stuck to the technical stuff, and although many were highly paid and respected, they simply were not held in as high esteem as managers.

"Our decision was to move all of the managers out of the top of the organizational structure and put them in the middle of the circles," Jack explains. "The teams were run by professionals. The decision to do that immediately started the pot to boil."

On the positive side, the professionals formed immediate and strong links with each other and started to drive very quickly toward the needed technical solution. On the other side, the managers were at loose ends. It was clear they were superfluous, so they did everything in their power to obstruct the program and show their worth. They introduced new measurement programs to chart the development of the new project, and they scheduled meetings over the smallest of things. The program ground to a halt as they worried about their roles in the new structure.

Of the eleven managers, four eventually emerged as active, aggressive and close to the professionals. Younger, and until recently professionals themselves, the four were comfortable with the new circles arrangement. The other seven were another matter. They found themselves under attack from two directions—the professionals and their four colleagues. They clearly felt underemployed, fearing they would be bypassed up the organizational ladder by their peers once the project was completed. Progress on the development program virtually stopped as a result of their angst, and Jack started to get profoundly worried.

"We had taken a real risk with this project; now I was faced with the fallout. This was an extremely high-profile program. If it failed, my career would be on the line. There was no doubt that there wasn't anyone anywhere who would 'understand' if the project failed. The rest of the company was working off the old model, and this new crazy approach was not going to be understood.

"People were stopping work and getting enmeshed in discussions about what the managers were doing, and where the role of the professional stopped and the manager began," Jack added.

Jack was constantly being besieged by men and women worried about their jobs, their status and the future in general. Indignation in the management group ran high.

"Some managers were complaining to H.R. that the rules were being flouted, and that was exactly what I didn't need," Jack said. "The last thing I wanted was the company searchlight on me. It would take a year of my life to explain myself."

As word of what Jack was doing leaked out, managers from other labs started getting nervous about dealing with his professionals, who were purporting to be able to make manager-type commitments on the project.

"It was simply a break of the 'officer' cadre concept, for a nonmanager to make a managerial decision," Jack says. "As a result, some managers passed a rule that a manager had to be present whenever departmental decisions were made. It was like being forced to take Daddy along to meetings. It was an insult. Altogether the project was falling apart, and my older, more experienced guys were on my case to go back to the tried-and-true way before disaster struck."

He didn't. He decided to bet everything on his frontal assault. He was going to charge uphill into enemy fire. His weapon of choice? Empowerment.

EMPOWERMENT: ARMING THE PEOPLE

"This was where the TQM program really fell into place," Jack explains. "We would do the program, but we would stress empowerment. That would force the debate on the structure, and on the role of the managers and professionals."

"The way we did it was simple. We ran each workshop as planned, and where we had a general discussion on empowerment with most groups, we had a very pointed discussion on roles with the eighty-person group that was running this project."

The word spread fast. Many people had been watching the development team with interest—it isn't every day that some part of the company tries to do something unprecedented—and so interest around the outcome of sessions was intense.

And the outcome was a revolution.

As we worked through the material, and the work that each part of the lab had to do, it became dramatically obvious that what Jack had known all along was true: There were simply too many managers.

The developers wanted to be led by their peers—the

professionals. They wanted there to be a few managers to handle administration and the interaction with the other labs, to serve as ambassadors to the rest of the company. But they wanted to take responsibility for their own work.

Jack now had to make a judgment call about his own role. In common with the majority of people who would be going to dispersed circles, or molecules, he was unsure what was left for him to do, or what exactly it was he should do.

"The big question was this: Did I step in and cut the number of managers, or let them work it out for themselves?" he recalls. "This question started to haunt me. If I were to step in, would they then become dependent on me? Would they stop growing as a team? If I did not step in, would they fall apart and put the whole program into even further jeopardy? There was no real guidance. No one in engineering had ever done what we were trying to do. I wasn't certain about what I should do."

Our recommendation was to step in, cut the management pool from eleven to five and then step back out again. Our logic was that Jack's role in the new molecular organization should be strategic, and the deployment of (human) resources was a strategic decision.

"It took me a couple of months to work this out for myself," Jack says. "But I finally came to the conclusion that I should be the one to take the managers out. The decision was immensely cathartic for me, and the organization.

"The small management team that was left forged strong bonds with the professionals, and they redistributed the traditional roles. The result was that I had hybrid professionals and managers, something that existed nowhere else in the business."

Things started to pick up speed, and the first delivery dates for the product were met.

Then Jack and Dave shot themselves in the foot.

REVERTING TO TYPE

"We were making real progress on the technical issues. But what we were working on was much more than a pure engineering project. There were business issues around brand management involved. We would be in charge of introducing the product into the marketplace, something we had never done before, and we had to start getting into more sophisticated business thinking than we were used to."

But as the surviving managers, along with the professionals, started working on the strategic issues, they found they were having problems making decisions. The problem centered around a problem of hierarchy. Previously, the most senior managers made the decisions. Now they were running the project as a team. How should they decide things? When they couldn't agree, how should they manage conflict? Who was supposed to make the final decision?

As a slow paralysis crept over them, one of the managers —the most senior in the traditional hierarchy—started to worry and wanted to make decisions unilaterally. The idea of working in teams was falling apart, and the project again looked threatened. Jack's answer was to ask Dave to take soundings. But that just added to the problem. Jack had shown a willingness to intervene—in his decisions to cut the number of managers on his own—and so Dave's questions took on an investigative flavor from the old world. In spite of that, or maybe because of it, what he learned was the group felt there was a need for more "teamwork training."

With so much riding on the project, Jack reacted immediately and sought out team training from a reputable behaviorist company. Everyone loved the training, but a combination of new roles, and uncertainty about the future, sent many of them off into a swamp of emotions. They got in touch with their feelings and out of touch with the business issues. The result was a major loss in productivity. And still the fundamental issue of who was in charge had not been decided.

What resulted was a project that was completely polarized. There were those who wanted to continue going "groupie," as the Molecular movement was started to be (affectionately) known, and those who wanted to revert. Some work was being done, but not much.

Jack was now seriously worried. The more he thought about it, the more paradoxical it all seemed. He had broken down the superstructure. The span of control was now better than twenty people per manager as more people came to work on the project, more than double the proportion of before. Plus, the boundaries between managers and professionals had been redrawn. People had more training in teamwork than you could shake a stick at and still the project was in jeopardy.

What was to be done? Why weren't they working as a team?

THIS IS A BUSINESS

What Jack was seeing was the old culture collapsing, the old bonds of doing business being pulled away. The new pillars of the Molecular Organization were not yet completely in place, and so the old culture began to tumble inward. In the old world, the managers made decisions and ran everything. All the developers—the people who actually did the work—had to do was, well, develop. They did not have to make business decisions. And in fact they didn't have to make many technical decisions either. They made recommendations to the managers, and the managers decided. The company looked after them.

In short, they lived in a very paternalistic environment.

In the new environment—with its fewer people and

shared decision making—there was a broader base of people involved in arriving at a decision, yet no one was feeling responsible for driving the business. The old model, bad as it was, at least provided a sense of accountability. There was always someone to blame if things went wrong. Some member, or members, of the Molecular model would have to be held accountable. And the team that had to be held accountable was "leadership," i.e., the old managers and new professionals. Yet these were the people who were avoiding that role by asking for more and more discussion and training.

Jack was again confronted with the problem of what to do. Should he step in and make decisions? Wait the group out? What?

"I decided that stepping in this time would be wrong," Jack concluded. "In the earlier case, when I decided to eliminate a number of managers, I was cutting resources that belonged to engineering as a whole. My stepping in there was legitimate. If I were to step in now, I would not be making a strategic decision, but an operational one, and operational decisions needed to be made by the group."

That was fine, but someone needed to make decisions.

"I eventually decided on a very no-nonsense approach," Jack explains. "It was basically a carrot and stick. I created bonuses for successful performance, and I made it clear that failure was career threatening. That was somewhat against my character, but time was short, and they had to understand that there were real world consequences to what they were doing."

Jack was treading a fine line now. Threats were anathema to H.R. But here he was lucky. Times were changing, and in its creaky way, human resources was beginning to see the writing on the wall for the old world. As the number of employees leaving the company steadily increased in the late 1980s and into the 1990s, the H.R. department had taken to doing extensive exit interviews.

What they found was the people the company most wanted to keep were frustrated by all the bureaucracy and red tape that had sprung up. They wanted more responsibility and a chance to get closer to the customer. In short, they wanted all the things that Jack was providing. As a result, H.R. was taking a more lenient view of Jack's aggressive behavior. Jack reckoned he had a window, and it was worth the risk of threatening people to get things done.

"In fact, I needn't have worried. The managers were as frustrated as I was. But because no one had called them on their behavior, they had no excuse for stopping the 'touchy-feely' stuff that was going on."

The effects of Jack's ultimatum were immediate and spectacular. There was one cathartic meeting of the management group, where the "senior" manager tried to kill the Molecular Organization once and for all.

"All this 'team stuff' is getting in the way of the project," he said. "The other managers don't have the experience or skills to push it through. The project needs someone with those skills. I will lead it."

The reaction was devastating. The rest of the team turned on him and let him know in no uncertain terms that they were not prepared to tolerate that idea. Those days were past, and his nominal seniority was an anachronism. Either he joined the team, them, or he could leave. They were simply not going to cooperate otherwise.

He suddenly saw the full implication of empowerment, a concept for which he had been a consistent champion. His job, as he had traditionally seen it, was on the line.

The manager was shattered. He collapsed into tears. Everyone was horrified. It was as if a mountain had fallen. Each one saw starkly the implications of what was being done to the old guard. Traditional ideas of status to go with a title would lose their meaning.

As someone said, "How could an assistant vice president

go home, and say he had lost his title? How could his wife and children understand what a 'senior team member' did." All the social reference points of the old paradigm were disappearing.

They gathered around him, and in taking stock of his pain took stock of their own. The result was a new maturity in the team.

"You can't keep an event as spectacular as that secret," Jack says. "It was round the organization in hours, and after the initial surprise, people started to understand the chasm between the old world and new one. They began to understand that things would never be the same again."

And they weren't.

For one thing, the program went full steam ahead, being completed in record time, despite the problems of the early days. But not without some more bumps. The senior managers who had tried to scuttle the program had been right. The others didn't have some of the basic skills needed and Jack had to step in to provide direction and training before the project was finally wrapped up.

For another, Jack stopped being a guerrilla fighter within his own company. He went from being someone who had to hide what he was doing to a regular speaker on empowerment and teamwork. Managers, who once fought those concepts with every fiber of their being, were suddenly desperate to learn more about them. They constantly called Jack to have him talk to their people, telling them what he had done.

And equally important, the manager/professional issues died in a gale of laughter. In a planning session where one manager kept talking about "managers and professionals," a senior and highly respected professional spoke up and said, "In a development organization, there aren't managers and professionals, only professionals and nonprofessionals."

This gentle reminder of the purpose of a development organization—to develop new products—punctured the balloon of managerial self-importance forever.

"The experience of making these changes was incredible," Jack says. "Once you have had a shot at such a change, there's no way you can go back to the humdrum life of running a department. I guess at one level my decision to take early retirement, and to go off and try to do it all again somewhere else, is indicative of the fun I had. Though it certainly didn't seem much like fun at the time."

Lunch was over. We shook hands and he walked out of the restaurant. It's not every day you have lunch with a war hero.

STAGE 2 GOLDEN RULES

• Customer—guide in the swamp

Teamwork training is crucial for building fundamental skills in the molecular world, but it must never be allowed to become an end in itself—or you can end up in the swamp. The best way to make sure that this happens is to focus on the business purpose—serving the customer.

• James Bond had the right idea

Not all change has to start with the top of the organization. But if it doesn't it takes people like Jack to make it happen against all odds. For them to succeed they have to work underground and find ways to bend the rules. The more people who know about what is happening, the greater the chance of being stopped.

• See the big business picture

Jack's developers couldn't see themselves as a business. They had no training in thinking about issues in "business" terms. This lack of business perspective is very common and extends right up to the top of corporations where specialists will have little comprehension of how the whole business works. In this early stage, the processes of thinking about the business should aim at building that skill.

Mass Customization Springs Ault Foods from the Commodity Trap

About the last place you would expect to find a clue to the new world of management is in the dairy industry. As the saying goes, "Milk is milk is milk." Most dairies have been handed down in the family for generations, and most people commonly hold the view that the industry is what it is, and cannot fundamentally change.

And it is not inherently obvious how the industry should change. There are no readily apparent sources of competitive advantage. Milk, the raw material, is bought at pretty much standard prices from the same cows. There is no opportunity to corner the market on Guernseys, and no way to patent a new udder. The product is then pasteurized with equipment that comes from the same suppliers, after which it is sold to the same stores who have the same customers. The playing field is pretty much the same for everybody.

There was something that set Ault apart from the crowd, however. The management team was highly entrepreneurial and had a culture that valued experimentation and innovation—traits that took them to Stage 3. Ault discovered the economics of mass customization. They are applying this knowledge to their commodity business as they seek to break the mold of price competition and razor thin returns.

We were the après-ski entertainment, and to be kind, it was a tough crowd.

Here we were, two visitors who could barely tell you which part of a cow gave milk, and we were supposed to explain to the senior executives of Ault Foods, probably the largest dairy in North America, how they could run their business better.

Terrific.

To make matters worse, six executives—from mass marketing powerhouses such as Pepsi and Procter & Gamble—had recently been hired by Ault to do just that, and they had yet to deliver.

These new managers had been spread like butter across the top of a very traditional loaf. The average length of service of the next layer of management down below them was over twenty years. There were several hundred managers who had seen their careers go dead the moment the hotshots arrived. Their assumptions of a steady rise to the top—with its traditional raises, perks and status—were crushed. They were not happy. They were not cooperative. And the new guys couldn't do without them. They had no idea how to make yogurt. They couldn't age cheese. We were told repeatedly as we prepared for the session that people wondered what these guys could do other than look at computer printouts. Clearly, there was no love lost.

Meanwhile, the new executive team wasn't all that fond of the old cheese makers.

"Look at the numbers," they told us. "This was fourteen businesses pushed together in name but not in fact. They haven't made a business out of it. They should stick to making cheddar and leave the real business to us."

There wasn't much conflict between the groups for the simple reason that they never really met. Senior executives, who held all the power, were based in the head office. They scattered memos like violets when they went out into the field, into the deeply rural areas.

And there they were met by craftsmen, men who could make the best yogurt and cheese you ever tasted, men who saw the group from headquarters as people who were planning to shut down their dairies, the places where these craftsmen had spent their lives.

No wonder there was hostility.

And we were supposed to bridge the gap.

We had been approached by one the new executives, Mike Ramsey, vice president of new business development, and a genuinely nice guy. Mike had a problem. He had just finished a three-day workshop, looking for new business opportunities, and he had come away depressed. Not that there hadn't been opportunities. Far from it. Over thirty-six had been identified, everything from new flavors of yogurt, to producing pints of "gourmet" ice cream. The problem? All

138 TOPPLING THE PYRAMIDS

the ideas were too small. None of them would boost significantly the company's net margins, which were hovering around 1.5 percent, and certainly none of them would revitalize the company. And the company was in desperate need of revitalization.

Thanks to aggressive cost cutting, Ault had just finished a year its then parent, Labatt Brewing, had characterized as "adequate." But now no one was pretending that cost cutting could continue. All the fat was gone, and still margins were slim to the point of extinction. Price wars were endemic, and continuous, in all product lines. And the chairman, Graham Freeman, was under pressure from Labatt, and he didn't like pressure. Not one bit.

Freeman is a big strong former hockey player with a straightforward approach to management. The goal's down there. The puck's up here. How do we get the puck from here to there? This was a man not used to, and not about to get used to, failure. He had volunteered to fix the problems at Ault and he wasn't going to fail—alone. If he was going down, he would take his new executives, including Mike, with him.

Mike understood that. What he couldn't understand was the reaction he had gotten to his ideas. He knew these people. He was as good as any of the new people Graham had brought in, but he also had small-town roots. He understood the dairies.

Still, the reaction to every single idea he had suggested varied between sullenness and aggression. It didn't matter what idea he brought up, both sides—the executives from headquarters and the traditional dairy men—couldn't wait to beat up on it and him. In a fit of black humor, Mike realized that this was probably the first time in two years the groups hadn't been at each other's throats. After his presentation, they had agreed unanimously. Not one of his ideas, his "specialized market opportunities," had enough volume to keep the machines going for five minutes.

And they were right. None of his ideas would produce significant volume, but they were the only ideas that were out there. All the long-run, big-market ideas were already subject to staggering competition. Besides, it was those high-volume, low-profit products that had gotten them to this point, a point where they were desperately scrambling to shave hundredths of a cent off their price. Those were the ideas that Mike and the rest of the new executives that Freeman had brought in were supposed to top.

Unless something changed radically, and soon, life at Ault was going to be hell.

Ironically, both sides were thrilled with the thought of the coming inferno. Sure, the old guard said, the company was going through tough times, but that just proved that they really needed us. Can't make cheese without a master cheese maker, you know.

The new executives felt the same perverse thrill. "When this year's numbers come in, those guys in the factory are really going to get it. Don't they know that we're 30 percent over capacity, in an industry that is 50 percent over? I'll do the best I can, but in the end it's those guys who have to change."

The chairman looked at this situation, and based on a logic all his own, decided that this was the perfect time to take everyone skiing. Last year had been rough, but everyone had done their best to cut costs. This year was going to be a bear, so why not give everyone a break now, mix some business with pleasure and take the senior managers, and their spouses, to a Rocky Mountain ski resort?

We would be the après-ski entertainment.

We'd be on for two hours for two consecutive afternoons, sandwiched between the time the slopes closed and pre-dinner drinks. We'd talk for just long enough for the spouses to do some shopping and get dressed for the evening.

The situation wasn't promising, but it may have been the best spent four hours of après-ski in history. It changed the company. Working together we created a revolution that sprang Ault from the "commodity trap."

It didn't start out that way.

We had been hired to present to the group the ideas in Michael Porter's *Competitive Advantage*. Graham is probably the best-read businessman we have ever worked with. He's a man who can glean ideas from what he reads and figure out ways to use those ideas to Ault's advantage. He wanted his managers to take the central themes from *Competitive Advantage,* which was the prevailing bible on how to compete, and apply them to the everyday business of running the dairy.

Porter had reduced his theories to two simple ideas: the value chain and the competitive matrix. To be fair to him, his book said much more, but it was rare then—or now—to find anyone who remembered anything else.

The value chain was Porter's term for the extended business enterprise. Traditionally, Porter argues, when we talk about corporations, we only look at the middle of the chain, the business itself. We don't consider the subcontractors and suppliers at one end, and the retailers/distributors/wholesalers at the other. And that, Porter argued, is wrong. To fully understand how a company does business—especially when it comes to finding ways to cut costs—you have to look at every single link in the chain. That was Porter's first idea.

His second, the competitive matrix concept, boils down to this: Companies can either be low-cost—that is, they can supply a needed product or service at the least expensive price—or they can be differentiated, i.e., they can give customers reasons to pay more for their product. Porter implies it is difficult, or impossible, to be both differentiated and low cost.

Graham was looking for a teacher. Someone who would use the après-ski time to drill Porter's ideas into the heads of his team. Based on Mike's recommendation, we were the "professors" of choice.

The first thing we did was go out and buy the book. And then, having read it and figured out what Porter was trying to say, we interviewed all the managers who were going on the ski trip and decided to tell a completely different story. The story of the "commodity trap."

THE "COMMODITY TRAP"

Milk is a high-volume business with relatively few players, but enough to create real competition. The machines that make milk are purchased by dairies from a relatively few suppliers. That means that everyone has basically the same production potential. Milk quality and content are regulated by the government, so there is not much product differentiation. Supply prices do vary a bit, but in Ault's major markets the differences were not a meaningful source of competitive advantage. You really can't afford to be innovative, in terms of new ideas or line extensions. Innovation costs money that won't be recovered. Therefore, it is too risky to do anything new.

The result is an endless stream of "me-too" products crowding the supermarket dairy case. Or as people in the industry put it so well, "Milk is milk is milk."

"You can't get ahead in this business," Mike explains. "Take yogurt. We come up with a new flavor idea. We try it. People buy it. Two weeks later, the flavor suppliers have duplicated the taste and all our competitors are using it."

What Mike neglected to say is that it may have taken Ault six months to come up with that new flavor. All that work, and the idea is knocked off in two weeks. No wonder

people didn't try to do anything innovative in the dairy business. When you add all this up, you could see why milk, and
its by-products, were destined to become entrants in *The
Guinness Book of World Records* as the ultimate commodities.
You could also see why this traditional way of competing was
a recipe for competition on price and cost. Faced with the
prospect of selling a commodity, Ault Foods—like thousands
of companies before it—decided to go for volume.

You understand the logic.

If we can get volume, Ault managers said, we can spread
the fixed costs of the dairy over more units and presto! our
unit cost drops. Once that happens, we can cut our prices
and get more volume. In fact, if we can lower our unit cost
far enough to drive our competitors to the wall, we will gain
a bit of breathing room.

This was Ault's strategy, and the strategy of everyone else
in the dairy industry. What this means is when a price war
starts, you'd better start shooting. Otherwise you're through.
Your prices will be too high, and the supermarkets will just
stop buying from you.

Milk is a loss leader. Not many supermarkets make
much, if anything, on milk. Some take a thumping loss on it.
The supermarkets take full advantage of the dairy price wars,
caused by producers' attempts to gain increased market share,
and continually play one supplier off against the other. That,
of course, perpetuates and accelerates the price wars.

Result?

Disaster.

What you had was a competitive dynamic that left everyone a little poorer. No one wins. No one can get off the
carousel. We're all going under. In addition, it's a totally
miserable way of making a living. The depressing thing was,
there didn't seem to be any way out. None of the traditional
answers worked.

Consider the usual management responses to this type of situation:

• **Increase quality.** Make your product better than the other guy's. The problem with that is you must have quality in dairy products. People who get sick won't buy your brand again. It is virtually impossible to differentiate on quality in the dairy business.

• **Use shorter product cycles.** Introduce so many new products so fast that you overwhelm the competition. The problem with that, of course, is there were already untold flavors and textures out there. One more at the margin seemed pretty pointless, and the cost would be horrendous. Besides, even if you came out with frozen, lumpy macadamia nut yogurt, how much market share would you gain?

• **Buy your way to profitability.** "The feeding frenzy of the 1980s in consumer goods, culminating in Nestlé's purchase of Carnation, was driven by this search for growth," Graham said. "Buying other brands isn't really possible. The purchase premium is rising on the big brands. There are still little ones around, but they're too small to make a difference to our bottom line. The only consolation is that our competitors are in the same boat."

The outlook was bleak. Worse, given the competitive trap it was in, Ault was potentially very easy picking for retailers.

The only way to keep its plants fully humming would be for the company to start making private label goods for the supermarkets, restaurants and other customers it served. But while that would keep the plants running, it would make the company even more vulnerable on price. Once a supermarket, for example, knew Ault was dependent on it for the volume it needed to run its plants efficiently, the retailer would squeeze Ault on price until it hurt.

So look at the situation Ault was in: It was selling the ultimate commodity in a market awash in commodities. Graham understood that. That was why he was so intrigued with Michael Porter. If differentiation wasn't possible, then you had to be low cost. No, wrong, you had to be lowest cost. In a price war you had to be the last person standing.

How do you cut costs? Where do you start? After the price of materials—which was basically set by the government—the biggest cost in producing dairy products is labor.

Well then, "off with their heads!"

That certainly would be the macho thing to do, but it would not have been the smartest. Ault has many unions, and if Graham had gone round swinging a machete, he would quickly find himself in confrontation—which would have been a disaster.

"It doesn't take a rocket scientist to realize that with our razor-thin margins, any disturbance in production is a disaster," says Larry Morden, Ault's vice president of human resources. "We're totally unionized, and they are very strong unions. If we had started unilaterally making big cuts, they could have sunk us."

Still, Graham needed to cut costs, and the way he did it underscores why he may be the smartest business executive we have ever worked with. He realized that the concept of empowerment, which Ault had already introduced, was going to do the job for him.

Graham and Larry had introduced empowerment for solid people management reasons. By pushing authority further and further down the line, you put decisions closer to the action, serve the customer more effectively, and at the same time, give people a better feeling about their jobs. But what Graham and Larry had discussed was that empowerment was having real, directly measurable cost impacts.

"People down the line were taking more responsibility for running the business," Graham explained to us. "As they did, we needed a smaller labor force to do the same work. We were able to reduce the head count by attrition, which was acceptable to the unions in what they knew was a tough economic environment. They saw, accurately, better, more stable jobs for their members."

He figured empowerment was giving him a competitive edge on the human side, but now he needed to translate that advantage into a lower-cost-operational approach to the business. And that's where we came in. We would explain Porter's concept of how companies in commodity-like businesses had to be the low-cost producer. If we could get that idea across, Graham hoped that his managers would continue on their cost-saving ways.

This was really all we were supposed to talk about, in summarizing *Competitive Advantage*. After all, there was just no way Ault could deal with the other half of Porter's theory, the part that dealt with differentiating your product. There was no way that a product like milk could be differentiated—or was there?

THE SESSION

A warning to everyone willing to give advice for a living. If you're offered an après-ski gig, run. You don't get to enjoy the skiing. You're wondering about the session. You don't really enjoy dinner; you don't know anyone. And all your best lines get swallowed in the prevailing tiredness of the audience listening to your speech.

But then again, you may start a revolution!

We covered Porter, but much more. We told the senior staff at Ault why just low cost wouldn't work.

This story brought the message home. A few years ago

we were involved in selling a local warehouse in the auto parts industry. We walked around with the new owner on the first morning after the sale, and as he got to the receiving department, he counted the number of desks (twelve) and noted each had a phone and person sitting there.

"By lunchtime, I want eleven of those desks out of here," he said to the head of the department, and he walked out. Needless to say, by noon nothing had happened. The new owner came back after lunch with a pair of scissors and cut the headsets off eleven phones. Then he shoved the desks out into the hall!

The message is simple. In a mass production world, low cost is not a picnic. It borders on the sweat shop. If you can't hack that culturally, you are not going to win. If you can hack it, your company will end up with a sterile work environment where no one will really want to be. But that's okay. Odds are you won't live to see the results of being the ultimate low-cost supplier. Yours will be one of the heads rolling out the door, long before that day arrives.

The fundamental problem Ault faced, if it continued to compete on price, was that it would never get off the cost-cutting treadmill, no matter how clever Graham was. No matter how quickly his managers seized on things such as empowerment, Ault would never get a cost curve so effective its competitors couldn't chase them down.

It was a no-win game.

So we proposed something totally audacious. Why don't you, we asked, break the mold and be differentiated—with the extra margin that brings—and be low cost at the same time?

That woke them up. There's nothing like a paradox.

"Okay, wise guys," Graham said, "how do you do it?"

"Well," we said, "we'd like to work one at a time with each of your divisions, in order to build a consensus and let our ideas grow."

"No time," replied Graham. "I'll put my top managers, from throughout the company, in a room all at one time, and you'll get your ideas across then, or not at all."

STAND AND DELIVER

Sixty-five people in a room. The group had been selected to represent all constituencies, the old guard and the new. There would be six sessions, with homework, and we began as we always do, with a simple question: Who is your customer?

We start this way for a reason. Invariably, our clients have tried everything imaginable before they've thought about asking for help. By the time we get called in, they have cut costs and reorganized so many times that their people are dizzy. Along the way, factions develop, fingers get pointed.

We want them to start thinking outside of their traditional boxes and get past the finger pointing.

You have to get them to open up their minds before any significant change can occur. It is an absolute prerequisite. It is also very difficult, given what companies go through trying to adapt to a new business environment.

At some point during the process of trying to change a company, all minds lock into place. Either because the process is too hard to think about or they've been confronted with too many choices or they're simply exhausted, people seize one particular course of action and refuse to see any other alternatives. Before change can happen, you have to unfreeze their minds.

By having them concentrate on who their customer is, we give them a chance to think about their problem differently. If they can figure out who their customer is, they can set priorities. "X is important to our customer, Y isn't, so we'll put our resources behind X."

And in the process of determining who their customer is, it's possible to end all the internal bickering and create unity. Everyone can rally around serving the customer, if only they can figure out who—exactly—their customer is.

So we asked, "Who's your customer?"

All heads turned to Graham.

"The customer is . . . who you decide," he told the group.

We divided the managers along product lines—ice cream, yogurt, liquid milk, etc.—and sent them off to decide who their customer was.

They had, of course, three choices:

1. *An internal customer, like a salesman.* In this environment, you make the product, and then it is incumbent upon your company's sales force to sell it. If you decide that your customer is someone inside the organization, then your number one priority is making sure that you are supporting that person, or department, to the fullest extent possible.
2. *An intermediary.* This customer is the middleman between you and the ultimate consumer. For a car maker, the intermediary is the dealer. For some of Ault's divisions, the intermediary would be the supermarket; for others it would be a restaurant.
3. *The end user.* You target the ultimate consumer of your product. In the ice cream business, the best example of this is Ben & Jerry's. They spend all their time worrying about what their customers like (in terms of ice cream and social issues) and what they don't.

When you tell someone to go pick a consumer, inevitably they come back and say they want to concentrate on all three. They don't want to leave any money on the table.

While that sounds fine, it is not realistic.

First, if you concentrate on all three markets, you aren't going to serve any one of them well.

Second, there is just no way you can afford to put in place the infrastructure you would need to effectively serve all three markets.

You have to choose. This does not mean you are going to deliberately slight the two markets you don't select. Far from it. You will continue to serve them the best you can. However, you will spend the bulk of your time, energy and resources on serving your primary customer.

And it was up to these sixty-five managers to determine who those primary customers would be.

Independently of one another, all five groups decided on the intermediary. That made sense. There really wasn't an internal customer who could dictate Ault's fate, and it's just too hard—and too expensive—to reach the consumer directly. That left the intermediary as Ault's customer, be it the supermarket for the milk and yogurt divisions, or restaurants for the food service unit.

Next question. What does this customer of yours value?

The initial answer from almost everyone was price, and almost everyone was simply wrong.

Jeremy Hobbins, vice president of sales, understood that. "Supermarkets don't care about price," he told the group. "They care about profit. We have led them to believe that the only way to profit is through price. But it ain't necessarily so."

Another breakthrough. And a common one. The fixation on volume, in the hopes of driving unit costs down, in companies used to mass production makes it difficult for managers to see that there might be something other than a low price that a customer could value.

The only way you are ever going to know what your

customer wants is to ask him, so we sent all five groups out into the field to ask their customers exactly what they wanted from a dairy.

Back together four weeks later, each group reported, somewhat sheepishly, that price wasn't the number one concern of their customers.

Oh, sure, you couldn't be 20 percent higher than the competition. But the customer repeatedly said they valued such things as convenient deliveries—you couldn't bring your stuff into a supermarket on a Saturday afternoon when everyone was doing their weekly food shopping—and less handling of the stock, either to put it out on the shelves, once it arrived, or to send it back once it spoiled.

We had a starting point. But how could you provide the customized service the supermarkets said they wanted without losing money?

Let Graham pick up the story:

"The first problem was to get our people to realize that the old thinking wasn't going anywhere. I decided the easiest way to prove that was to walk them through the numbers. We started with yogurt. Yogurt is a commodity with very narrow margins, say, 1.5 percent. We were a poor third in the market, and we didn't seem to be able to break out, despite some clever marketing, where we got the rights to market Muppets yogurt to go after the kids' market. Our people had always assumed that we could not lick the cost problem without doubling our volume, and we couldn't double our volume because there just wasn't that kind of demand for yogurt. So we languished. We were going nowhere.

"The decisive moment came when we asked the people in finance to analyze our costs and compare them to the competition's. What a shock! The idea of competing on volume turned out to be based on a fallacy. Everyone believed the more volume we pushed through, the lower our costs. In fact, we believed that so deeply that no one had ever run the numbers.''

When they did, they found that over 70 percent of the production cost of yogurt is milk. And the price of milk was the same for everyone. Double the volume and, at best, you might take off a cent on each container.

The shock was palpable, and it just got worse as the company realized that the mass production myopia did not stop with the finance department. It went all through the company, up to and including manufacturing.

Graham again: "Yogurt was made in long runs. We'd do a run of peach, then clean out the lines, and then do a run of raspberry. We'd clean out the lines again, and then do some other flavor, and so it went. Each flavor was sent off to cold storage and would stay there until we had enough variety to fill an order. Supermarkets always order a shipment of mixed flavors. They'd want twenty cases of strawberry, fifteen cases of peach and maybe six of coffee.

"The logic for operating the way we always had was irrefutable. We needed the long runs to get the volume to the point where we could lower our unit costs."

But as we've just seen, Ault now knew there really wasn't anything to be gained by doing long runs. If long runs didn't add anything, would short runs really cost anything? That was the question we had, and perhaps because it had been such a tough assignment, we got to thinking about having a drink.

One of the interesting things about bars is that they can make you a drink at a touch of a button. The bartender picks up a wand, which is attached to a series of hoses, and he can put ginger ale, club soda or tonic into your glass simply by touching the right button on the wand.

Couldn't you do that with yogurt? After all, all yogurt

starts with the same plain base, and the flavors are added in at the last minute. Couldn't you have a dozen hoses on the line, and squirt in at will the flavors you needed?

"Why, yes," the dairy men said. The technology was available to do exactly that.

"But," the managers asked, "don't we need those long runs of strawberry, chocolate or whatever to keep our costs down?"

"Well, of course, once we realized how little we were saving on the long runs, we understood that we didn't need to do them at all," Graham said. "In fact, when we looked at the economics of continuous production of variety, they were truly staggering.

"The new approach meant we could produce to order, and we could cut out the cold storage, which is very expensive.

"But the real kicker was, by producing custom orders, we could deliver fresher yogurt."

Yogurt, as anyone who lets it sit in the refrigerator too long learns, has a limited shelf life. Ault's research had come up with preservatives that could extend that life to a maximum of forty days. In the old system of long production runs, Ault used twenty-five of those days up on average just getting the yogurt from cold storage into the stores. As a result, the yogurt could only be on the supermarket shelf for fifteen days, and not really that long, since toward the end of its forty-day life, yogurt separates and looks unpleasant.

No wonder Ault was ending up with 5 percent returns on a product that only had a 1.5 percent margin!

"Under the new way of producing, we could get the yogurt to the stores within twenty-four hours. That meant it could sit on the supermarket shelf for up to thirty-nine days, instead of fifteen," Graham said. "Our return rate might drop to zero, and our profits may get out of the ditch!"

Amazing, but true. It could actually be cheaper to produce customized orders than to follow the old mass production techniques.

Ault never would have understood that if they hadn't first figured out who their customer was and then stopped to determine exactly what that customer wanted. Without doing both those things, they would have gone around and around the same old treadmill.

The central message of Ault is simple. You can be differentiated and low cost at the same time. Indeed, in a world of niche markets, you must be.

But the insights did not stop with yogurt. Once the sixty-five managers understood the breakthrough, they could see how it applied to their other operations.

The production runs in milk, for example, could also be customized for each store. But their understanding of the issues facing their customer went further. Understanding that supermarkets want deliveries kept to a minimum, Ault could deliver all dairy products on the same truck. After talking to their customer and learning that supermarkets, like all other companies, want to keep their labor costs to a minimum, Ault knew it could go further still. Milk could be loaded onto special racks that could be wheeled off Ault's trucks, right into the dairy case. No one at the supermarket need touch it all.

Let Jeremy Hobbins tell the story:

"As the milk goes through the dairy it gets handled all the time. It's taken in and out of refrigeration, put on dollies and trucks, loaded onto racks and so on. Well, the cost accountants reckoned that by the time all those costs, including the refrigeration costs, were added together, handling was the largest single cost in making milk after the milk itself."

"To get an idea of how important this discovery is, you've got to realize that inside the dairy, taking a fraction of a cent out of the cost of a gallon of milk makes you a hero, since you are dealing with so many millions of gallons per day. Take out a cent, and they will erect a statue to you, and here we had a chance to take out several cents of every gallon. All we had to do was eliminate all the handling!"

Now clearly that was impossible, but it gave everyone a goal to shoot for. And the easiest way to think of it was to use the yogurt example.

If milk could go down the line onto the truck and straight to the supermarket shelf, the stores would get fresher milk, handling costs would drop and refrigeration costs would shrink.

"This insight was fortuitous," Hobbins recalls. "We were just on the edge of a major investment in refrigeration and our minds were locked. The suppliers and the dairy engineers told us that for every so many millions of gallons of capacity, you need so many gallons of refrigeration. By producing milk to order, we could turn back from the brink of what could have been an expensive mistake." Ault had achieved this insight by realizing that mass customization does not stop at the point of contact with the customer. It allows a total rethink of the whole production cycle. When this happens, not only do you provide the customer with a differentiated offering, but you make inroads into your cost base too. It is the essence of mass customization, to be differentiated and low cost.

How did it all work out? The ideas generated at these sessions started a revolution in Ault which is still going on. The yogurt concept was the catalyst for rethinking all their operations, and as they make investment decisions, they are using a totally different mindset. Even more important, it gave focus to serving the customer. Today Ault seeks to mold its operations to its customers, to provide each one with exceptional service at a competitive cost base. Their success in increasing market share is testimony to their effectiveness.

ONE MORE THOUGHT

The Ault story is a story of a new technical paradigm, empowerment and strong forceful leadership. Graham had vision and stamina. The change process that kicked all this off was merely the catalyst to implementing his vision.

Ault is not alone. The idea of the batch of one, or mass customization, is spreading at enormous speed. It can now be found in all kinds of industries. Nothing is more powerful than an idea whose time has come.

There's the now famous story about a Japanese bicycle manufacturer who makes custom racing bicycles in about two hours. His competition takes six months.

How he does it is simple. The customer sits on an exercise bike in the store. They lock in how tall you are, how much you weigh, where your hands hit the handlebar and so forth, sending all the information electronically to the factory where a customized bike rolls off the line two hours later. Because you would find it impossible to believe that you could get a customized bike in two hours, they wait two weeks to ship it to you.

This story is being repeated in dozens of industries. McGraw-Hill will customize a textbook for a lecturer's specific course. Ethicon can customize packages of surgical instruments. Mass customization is well under way.

In many cases, it just requires a different way of viewing the problem.

STAGE 3 GOLDEN RULES

- **Not all customers are the same**
  Ault took a major step forward in focusing on the customer—choosing the intermediaries as the

source of competitive advantage. But they went one stage further. They realized that not all intermediaries are the same. There were clear differences between a supermarket and a restaurant, but equally clear ones between supermarkets, the corner store and the specialty food boutiques. Even within the world of supermarkets, some were leading-edge players and others very staid. Ault set themselves on a trajectory of learning more and more about their customers and feeding it back into the system.

- **Breaking out of "scale jail"**

In common with most managers, Ault's production experts had always thought in terms of economies of scale and large volume, or of craftsman-made custom lots at the other extreme. Breaking that mold was like breaking out of a jail —a jail of the mind. Once they started to see the world in mass customization terms, all kinds of things became possible. By taking this fresh approach they were able to move away from incremental reengineering of established systems and make a leap to a different cost base. The challenge that faced Graham was putting enough pressure on the organization so that the insights were not lost when the going got tough. For example, when the equipment suppliers did not come through, he hired a special "tinkerer" whose job it was to reconfigure various parts of the production system for flexibility.

- **Molding everything to the customer**

Ault reinvented their entire way of operating to meet the needs of many different classes of customers all at the same time. This involved changing the factories, the delivery routes, the marketing approaches, the sales force, the computer systems—everything about the business. This total rethinking of operations was unnerving for the people in the business—every job would change. To achieve this they had to subsequently install a process of involving everyone in the reinvention process, building understanding and buy-in.

IBM: Wrapping Around a Market

IBM is probably the most watched company in the world, with brand-name recognition second only to Coca-Cola. Over the years, IBM voyeurs had stood in awe at its seemingly unstoppable power, heralding it as perhaps the best managed corporation in the world. As a result, IBM became the cornerstone of every respectable stock portfolio. Now, however, IBM is scrambling to fundamentally reinvent itself while absorbing staggering losses.

IBM was trapped in a classic dilemma: the prison of success. It had been the paragon of marketing companies, as close to its customer as anyone could be. When that customer base started to fragment, IBM was faced with a managerial integration problem of colossal dimensions.

IBM is the world's largest general contractor. But unlike the guy who builds your house where it is constructed by individual handiwork, IBM must pull together thousands of solutions to meet the changing needs of millions of individual customers every day. And do it against the complexity of development labs, manufacturing, marketing, personnel and finance departments—strung out from New York to Tokyo to London.

IBM is wrestling with Stage 4 of becoming a Molecular Organization, re-creating its management system and structure to wrap it seamlessly around the customer. In Stage 4, organizations have to face the most profound changes in their management approaches. Generally, it involves a rethink of many accepted practices, including how to structure, how to compensate people, what the best routes to power are for ambitious people and many more. As IBM goes through its transformation, it is facing all of these. This is the story of the introduction of a new gene into the company which we believe will have profound long-term consequences as the company seeks to craft solutions for its customers on a mass basis.

Helping a giant organization change is like trying to move a pile of Jell-O. If you push on one spot, you fall in. The only way to move a Jell-O mountain is to push on several places simultaneously.

You'll see lots of pushing at IBM in coming years. That really is the best way to reshape the company, despite all the calls from people to break it up.

After IBM reached outside the organization, for the first time in its history, and appointed Lou Gerstner as chairman in early 1993, there were numerous calls to dismember the company. The argument was that by dividing the company up into smaller pieces, the corporation would become "lean and mean" and shareholder value would rise.

But proponents of this divide to conquer strategy fail to understand that it doesn't matter if IBM is one company, or fifty; the parts must still come together to serve the customer. Even more important, in a fast-moving market, it is a basic source of competitive advantage for IBM to be a unified company with a free flow of information internally about new product ideas. The problem is how you hold a mammoth company together and get it to act like one while still getting the speed and flexibility of a small player. Gerstner clearly understands this.

He captured the dilemma in a remark to shareholders in early 1993: "You can be too centralized and too decentralized. We ought to be able to drive down the middle of that road." What Gerstner didn't tell the shareholders was that the company had been experimenting with ways of achieving this for the past three years—and with considerable success.

This is a problem that IBM didn't used to have. In the old days, it knew exactly how to integrate those pieces: You focused on the customer. And indeed throughout its corporate history, IBM had been one of the most customer-focused organizations that the world had ever seen.

It didn't run into trouble because it took its eye off the

customer. IBM's woes are more basic than that. IBM started racking up losses in the billions because its customers had changed, and the company failed to change with them.

THE WAY IT USED TO BE

From the very beginning, IBM had been customer focused, and everyone in the company could tell you exactly who that customer was: the emerging Chief Information Officer (CIO). And as IBM's terrific growth from the 1950s through the 1970s showed, that was exactly the right person to concentrate upon.

But in the 1980s, the customer started to change. There was big battle within corporations about how the information processing function should be run. In the early part of the decade, the decision was that everything should be centralized. The CIO would coordinate all the information needs, make centralized buying decisions and then parcel out what was needed to the users. This corporate decision merely codified what had been happening all along, and, of course, played to IBM's strengths.

But then the personal computer came along and everything started to change. Suddenly, the potential to put intelligence in the hands of the user became irresistible. "Push everything out to the field" became the battle cry, and "everything" included computing. IBM was caught unawares. Not only was it focused heavily on mainframes, but it was also organized by product line. Now the customer was buying many different products from many different distribution systems, and many different parts of the business had to come together to provide a meaningful solution.

Now IBM had to be able to come together by customer type, not products. Customers in retailing or direct mail didn't care about the difference between mainframes and minis. All they knew was they had a computing problem that they wanted IBM to solve.

When IBM was growing to be a superpower in the 1950s, 1960s, and into the 1970s, scientific advances drove the computer market. There is no company on earth with better technological resources than IBM. (For example, the company has more Nobel laureates than any other firm.) So it is not surprising that IBM drove the computer market for decades with a technology no one could match.

But today technology doesn't give you an insurmountable advantage in the vast middle and low-end parts of the computing markets. Whatever hardware you need, you can buy off a shelf. Indeed that is how the prototype of one of the hottest personal computers, Compaq's Prolinea, was created. Compaq engineers literally went to computer supply stores, picked the components they wanted off the shelf, and built the first Prolinea in six weeks.

What now drives the vast majority of the computer market is a company's ability to focus its technological strengths on precisely what its customers need today, and more important, what those customers will want tomorrow.

IBM had not responded quickly enough to this changing market. Instead, it kept relying on an old image of the customer, and as a result was steadily losing market share and money. The company reported a $4.9 billion loss at the end of 1992, financial results that led to the resignation of Chairman John Akers and the subsequent hiring of Gerstner.

For IBM to regain supremacy, it needed to change. Specifically, the company needed to:

• **Develop a clear market positioning for each different customer set.** The company needed to answer for the thousands of new customers that were springing up, "What does IBM stand for?" The old CIOs could answer that question easily, but as we have seen, the CIOs were no

longer IBM's only customer. And even the CIOs were
changing as they tried to respond to the needs of their internal customers.

• **Be able to work seamlessly across geographical,
product, industry group and other boundaries to serve
the customer.** Customers don't care how your company is
organized. If they have a problem, they don't want to hear,
"It's not my department." They want you to resolve the
problem—now! This, of course, ties back to the first point.
IBM, which had always presented itself as a craftsman, would
have to convince its new customers, who were often building technology departments for the first time, that it could
also function as a general contractor.

• **Have a business orientation, rather than a functional one,** a concept that builds directly off the previous
point. Most people who work in companies view their
world from a "functional" or "product line" perspective.
They look inward. They are either marketing people or finance people. No one it seems is a businessperson anymore.
That just won't work in today's world. You have to look
outward toward the customer. You have to see your job as
taking care of his or her needs. If you don't, it is a prescrip-
tion for failure, as IBM learned the hard way.

To truly understand where IBM was, is, and will be going, it helps to spend a couple of minutes discussing the
world the company grew up in. Since IBM is a technology-
based company, it is not surprising that systems theory is an
important part of the organization. One of the theory's underlying tenets says that if a subsystem is to survive within a
larger system, it must reflect, and link to, the complexity of
the larger system.

The subsystem can do that in one of two ways: either by
having the necessary complexity within it or by being set up

in such a way that it is able to connect with the complexity of the larger system.

IBM is a vivid example of this theory come to life.

IBM is an integrated company, operating across the entire computer market. A few years ago the computer market was relatively homogeneous. That's a fancy way of saying it was not complex. Today, obviously, computers have pervaded every aspect of our lives, and as a result have become more specialized. In fact, they have evolved so far that some don't even look like computers anymore. Your car has more computing power than a major corporation had not so many years ago.

As the complexity in the market grew, IBM, which was structured for a less complex world, was put under enormous stress. Its old way of doing business was strained to the gills as it tried to serve all the different market segments that developed. Suddenly, just making mainframes for a standard market wasn't enough, you needed to provide a host of different customers with mainframes, minis, PCs and a vast array of specialized software. And there were market segments within those market segments. This customer wanted to use a PC for strategic advantage, another was content to be a follower and wanted a strictly low-cost solution. This had an enormous impact on the mix of products being offered. Did customers want a basic PC, one with an internal hard drive, an external drive? Could you help them if they wanted to link all their personal computers together? How about if they wanted to establish hundreds of offices around the world? The company was not set up to deal with the fragmentation.

If that were not bad enough, niche competitors began springing up. They noticed the evolution of the market, and instead of trying to be like IBM, covering the entire waterfront, they dealt with the market complexity problem by just focusing on one slice of the pie. Apple became the "computer for the rest of us," and targeted the personal computing and education markets. Sun decided to concentrate on the workstations. Microsoft decided to own the user.

The result was, IBM was trapped. The market was demanding that the company change, and yet the very corporate structure that had served the company so well for so long wouldn't let in. Even worse, it was slow, inflexible and inward-looking. Plus it gave IBM a cost burden its niche competitors didn't have.

In its simplest form, a firm is a single niche company that provides its customers with a single offering. As it grows out of that simple state, it also grows in organizational complexity.

Consider Compaq, for example. It began by targeting business customers. Having done a good job in that market, it sought to grow by selling personal computers as well. That meant a new product line, and along with it came an increased cost structure, while organizational complexity rose along with its product lines. Ultimately if Compaq (or companies like it) keeps growing, it will enter IBM-land, where it offers a full product line in an attempt to serve every part of the market.

The cost of integrating all this complexity rises as the company moves further and further away from its simple state. Layer upon layer of organization is built to accommodate all this growth.

"We thought, of course, that we were adding value to the customer in excess of our cost of organizing," an executive told us. "But the result in the market showed that if this had ever been true, it no longer was."

IBM had painted itself into a corner by continuing to do business the old way in an increasingly fragmented market. It suddenly found itself competing with niche marketers who did not carry the complexity or the cost of managerial integration. Moreover, those niche players could achieve some of the product and market advantages of an IBM through partnerships and alliances with other firms that could be formed with a minimum of complexity—and cost.

If IBM was to remain big—and once again become profitable—it had a basic problem to solve. It needed to figure out how it could respond to a fragmenting marketplace, yet still take advantage of its size. This is a Stage 4 problem. It demanded that the traditional ways of doing things had to be replaced with a cooperative, low-cost system that would wrap this giant around many markets simultaneously. This meant a major rethink of how the company did business.

That is not an easy task. As we've seen, complexity grows with size. The more people and things in a system, the harder it is to both organize and manage them. And as the history of the Fortune 500 shows, the bigger the company, the slower it is to react to changing market conditions.

In biology there is an idea called allometric growth. It says that as an organism grows, the parts must grow in proportion. This theory explains how we know the size of a dinosaur from finding a single leg bone. The reasoning goes like this: The legs supported the body, so they had to be structurally able to do it. So given that the leg was so big, while knowing that legs tend to support so much weight, we therefore know the dinosaur must have been about yea tall.

The same sort of logic seems to apply to organizations. Given a certain corporate size, the accounting department, for example, that supports the business has to be so big. Unfortunately, that means so much cost. When the business environment becomes more competitive, and the organization can no longer support that cost, the system must change in order to be able to cut expenses. Otherwise, like a dinosaur that is too big for its legs, it will just topple over.

This in a nutshell explains the problem IBM is dealing with. It is trying to break down into smaller units to lower the cost of managing itself. But at the same time it is trying to remain a single entity. It is trying to be small while remaining big. Which is, of course, as good a definition of a large Molecular Organization as you could wish.

All this is much harder than it sounds. There seems to be an unwritten rule in business that says when a big company breaks down into smaller units, each of the new smaller divisions must replicate the old structure. The result? Instead of having one big pyramid, you get a series of smaller ones. That's what happened at IBM every time the company tried to reorganize and/or break up into smaller units. The company ended up with a series of small bureaucracies instead of one big one.

There is no guarantee that would change if IBM were to fracture into a series of small companies, as some critics are suggesting. The secret is not dividing up the company, but eliminating the bureaucracy. That's what the team IBM put on the problem had to do.

THE PROBLEM

We were approached by Stephen Vehslage, then head of IBM's education division, to try to find an innovative resolution to this vortex.

Stephen was not your typical IBMer. In a world of engineers he is a medieval historian. Deeply experienced in its overseas and marketing operations, Stephen was often given tasks that required "outside-of-the-box" thinking, and he had just been handed another one. His assignment: to break up and change the culture of the company. He had been asked by Terry Lautenbach, president of U.S. operations, to take on the role of changing IBM's management system to be more customer responsive.

This was an assignment Stephen readily accepted. Intensely loyal to the company, his aim as he put it was, "to leave IBM better than I found it."

In 1989, when we got there, it wasn't remotely better. IBM was still trying to deal with two radical change problems that Chairman John Akers had presented: The first was Akers's plan to make the company Market Driven, an idea which quickly evolved into the second program, Market Driven Quality (MDQ). The underlying thought behind both was simple: to get IBM beyond an obsession with products and technologies to an obsession with the needs of its customers, who, as we have seen, had changed.

Let's take a simple example of dot matrix printers. In its printers, IBM was using a small steel clip to hold the paper in place. To make sure that clip was of the highest quality, IBM machined it a total of five times.

In its printers, Hitachi used an aluminum clip that it bought off the shelf. They both worked just fine, and the customer could not have cared less about all the "quality" that IBM had engineered in.

You could see the same thing happening elsewhere in the company. IBM got busy eliminating "defects," while much of their equipment and software was not nearly as user-friendly as the competition's. Almost all the focus of improving quality was internal. It was rare if someone asked, "What does the customer think about all this?" In the old days, that question never had to be asked. IBM intuitively knew what its customers wanted. Now it didn't.

By the time Stephen called us, both market driving programs had bogged down in the complexities of the management system.

The problem was obvious to us, but not to the people who had spent their entire life working inside this corporate culture. IBM was just set up the wrong way to deal with its new customer base. IBM's management system was a classic pyramid. Key decisions were made centrally. Information was gathered at the lower levels and passed up through an extremely well defined chain of command. The information was interpreted at the top by the most senior managers of the company. They made decisions and passed their edicts down through the very ranks that had passed up the data.

That is typical of pyramid structure common to most large organizations at that time. What made IBM slightly different was that it also believed passionately in management by objective, which focuses accountability on individuals. That is fine in a simple world. You are given a goal, and you are then judged on how well you accomplish it.

However, with fragmenting markets and increasing competition, IBM's world was now anything but simple, and no individual could deal with the complexity. Teamwork was crucial—close teamwork—but the individualization of everything got in the way.

That was bad, but what was worse was the problem of dependencies that had been created in every IBM division. Dependencies occur, for example, when the personal computer operation needs a piece of software that is being developed by the folks over in mainframes. They negotiate an agreement ("You'll have it Tuesday") and record it as a dependency. Dependencies are supposed to be delivered against. In other words, if you give someone your word, you are expected to keep it. The trouble is that the dependencies become so complex—to deliver the software to the PC division, mainframes need to get the data from software, which in turn has to get the final numbers from marketing, who needs to hear from . . . —that the failure of any one division to deliver brought down the whole house of cards.

To give you an idea of the scope of the problem, one day

a senior manager in IBM's software lab in Toronto sat down to map all his division's dependencies company-wide. He soon ran out of space on the largest sheet of paper he could find, and later he found that there was no computer program sophisticated enough to catalog the dependencies.

Complex dependencies are a paradox. There is nothing wrong with having operations spread across the world. Indeed, to obtain local feel for products and services, that kind of dispersion can be desirable. The problem occurs when different organizations report to different places and each has a different set of priorities. Then good people acting with perfect goodwill end up in contention as they are pulled by different demands. As the market fragments, this gets steadily worse.

IBM had become exceptionally skilled at dealing with this problem. There was an elaborate process of discussion to get contentions solved. But such a process took time. As those fragmenting markets moved faster, niche competitors —not burdened with this problem—reacted ever more swiftly. Time was a luxury IBM did not have. IBM was increasingly a prisoner of its own organizational success, and the quality program had simply highlighted this problem.

IBM had tried to deal with the problem by restructuring. Endlessly.

"Like most businesses we'd recognized the need for cross-functional cooperation," Stephen explains. "We created 'matrix' organizations, where related groups were expected to work together in an attempt to cure the problem. But it didn't."

In fact, reorganization had become almost an annual affair. IBM, like many other companies, had tried just about everything: organizing by product line, by geographical area, by function, by industry group and so on. Each reorganization solved minor problems but also created new ones (like turf wars). Even worse, this constant shuffling of boxes on the organization chart continuously disrupted the organization.

All these reorganizations took time. That was time not spent dealing with the new customer base that was evolving. More important, the endless reorganizations did not address the fundamental problem of making IBM more responsive to the customer.

The reasons for that were threefold. First, the company existed as a three-dimensional matrix, if you were to sketch out what was really going on within IBM. The company was organized by product group, function and geography. This created horrendous complexity.

Second, to get around this complexity, IBM, during its reorganizations, would decide to have all three axes report to one of them, but this just created uncertainties and new areas of contention. Who do you go to if you have a problem? Who is your real boss?

Seeing that reorganization number 18 was not working, someone would design reorganization plan 19, and the matrix would be flipped again. And again. And again.

But no matter how many times they reorganized, the pyramid management structure still remained; it was part of every solution. That was just the way IBMers viewed organizational life at that time. You started with a pyramid.

The result of all this constant turmoil was that people were hopelessly torn in their loyalties. They really wanted to do a good job for their customers and their colleagues, but they still had to satisfy the internal needs of the business— and those tended to take precedence.

Self-interest, contradictory measurements and distance from both the boss and the customer had all combined to make the matrix largely unworkable. Something had to change.

BACK TO BASICS

After a couple of months studying the problem, Stephen knew what he was up against. He spent a while making various attempts to prod the organization along, but he had little to show for his efforts. IBM kept going along as it always had, and it kept losing market share. Totally frustrated, Stephen called us.

After talking to everyone involved in senior management, it was clear that we had to get IBM away from its traditional way of doing business. As long as there was a pyramid, and various matrixes, nothing was going to change.

Market Focused Communities (MFCs) became the lightning rod of the change we helped implement. But it took us a while to get that idea across.

The concept itself is relatively simple. Markets are like a box of iron filings. If you throw a magnet into the box, the filings will naturally group around the magnet. The idea was to find the big magnets, market segments, and attach to them market focused communities.

That was what we wanted IBM to do: organize naturally. The vehicle would be MFCs, which are teams of key line people who have the responsibility for serving a particular market. Based on a vision of what they think their customer values, the teams create the entire strategy for dealing with their markets. The MFC is a self-contained unit. It coordinates its activities directly, so that it is able to present a consistent face to its customers and market.

To make this concept work, everyone must be committed to satisfying the needs of the customer. This is not a group of people who get together to talk shop. It's an action group, and one that has the authority to get things done. Two of the key questions asked of anyone who wants to join the group are: "Are you real?" and "Do you have the authority to change things?" The answers have to be yes, because you must commit to making something happen once the group decides that change is needed. If you don't have that ability, members of the MFC ask, "Then why are you here?"

Limiting the MFC to only people who could get things done represented a major change in IBM's corporate culture. Like many companies, people at IBM frequently attended meetings just to remain in "the loop." It was the way they could keep up-to-date on what was happening, whether or not they were directly involved.

The problems with that are twofold. One, the more people you have in a room, the longer it takes to get anything done. This reason is directly related to the second factor. It seems to be a law of human nature that people who attend a meeting feel compelled to offer advice, ideas, background or "maybe this is a crazy suggestion but," whether or not they understand what is being discussed.

MFCs dealt with this problem directly. If you didn't have the authority to help the group move toward its goal, you were politely asked to leave.

In addition, the community is forbidden from having its own staff, beyond a single person responsible for fixing meeting times, setting agendas, writing minutes, etc. (i.e., the group secretary). With MFCs there is to be absolutely no new bureaucracy. If work is to be done—for example, a study is needed—then each interested participant should volunteer people for a self-liquidating task force.

To make sure the MFC works efficiently, a Market Opportunity Manager (MOM) is appointed. The MOM is responsible for bringing the group together, and making sure all the necessary people are at the meetings. The MOM runs the meeting and takes the group's concerns to senior management.

Initially, MFCs are empowered by top management, but rapidly they take on a life of their own. A fundamental measure of the communities' effectiveness is how much they can accomplish on their own without going back to management to resolve differences. Indeed, to the extent that they do have to go back to management to resolve a conflict or make a decision, they have failed.

It is important to emphasize that the MFCs are not just another management buzzword. They are an organic structure that builds on the "paths where people walk."

As we have seen, the way things really get done in organizations is through informal networks. Projects for the most part get accomplished in spite of the formal systems, not because of them.

IBM, like other major organizations, really operated on the "thousand-pound gorilla" principle that we talked about in the first chapter. People with strong personalities take charge and get things done. Market focused communities merely allowed these natural patterns of working to rise to the surface and overcome most traditional bureaucratic barriers.

What holds the MFC group together is not a series of rules and bosses, but values. Not soft values based on humanistic concerns. But rather a common belief in what it will take to satisfy the customer.

The result of accepting this new form of management is that IBM has introduced a new gene: the concept of self-directed top management teams grouped around the customer. Before, people at the top of the company competed with one another. Now they are cooperating and deciding on their own what needs to be done.

The self-regulation and self-management aspects of MFCs cannot be overemphasized. They represent a fundamental shift of the traditional management paradigm. That shift is even underscored by the language we used. We call MFCs a community because the word has no connotation of hierarchy.

At first, it was like pulling hens' teeth just to make people take the idea of MFCs seriously. Many resisted overtly or, worse, passively. The only thing we had going in our favor was that IBM's management had tried just about everything else and still the company was getting its clock cleaned.

PILOTS AND PROTOTYPES

Introducing an idea into a company the size of IBM is fundamentally different from working with a small organization. Change problems seem to become different every time the organization becomes about ten times bigger. If you want to change a business of one or two thousand people, you can devise a program that will reach everyone directly. The CEO can still talk to or be seen by every person in the business. The sense of intimacy and the speed with which the change can be implemented are both very high.

Move up in size to the twenty thousand plus range, and the problems change shape. The CEO can no longer be seen directly by everyone. The change has to be delivered using a much wider range of leaders, each of whom must have bought in first. This requires the formation of a more broadly committed leadership team at the center of the business and ensures that they are truly on board before anything is done.

When you get up to two hundred thousand plus you are dealing with a political system the size of a small city, with major geographical, ethnic and business diversity. A head-on approach in this case leads to major resistance, but resistance that is largely submerged. This is the world of "compliance"

—respect for and acceptance of authority. In this world, resistance is rarely overt. People take what is given, then go through a calculus of their own. Some love the idea and comply wholeheartedly. Others are indifferent and simply comply. But it is realistic to recognize that others will see nothing in it for themselves and indulge in malicious compliance—essentially saying they are complying but doing varying degrees of the opposite. The goal here is to win the hearts and minds of the people so that they will come with you—by answering the fundamental question "What's in it for me?"

Answering this question turns out to be difficult in something as nebulous as an organizational change based on communities that wrap around the customer. It is not intuitively obvious what advantage any individual will gain, nor is it enough to assert the need to be customer focused. The answer in IBM's case was interesting—less work!

This was not an easy sale. Creating the communities would demand a lot of effort and even arm twisting to get people to attend the early sessions. How would it lead to less work? The answer lay in the fast-moving and fragmenting market. Everyone was thigh deep in contention as they tried to react to fast-shifting circumstances. That contention took up tremendous amounts of time and energy and deeply frustrated all IBMers who simply wanted to do a good job. What we promised was that the market focused communities would bring focus to their efforts and allow them to come to broad strategic agreements that would eliminate a large part of the misunderstandings on which the contentions were based. In short, MFCs would make their lives easier and lower the amount of "useless" work they found themselves doing. Most were skeptical. But the idea sounded reasonable on the surface, so it was worth a shot. The next question was how to roll out the idea.

The key to rolling out a concept in a company as big as

IBM is to see the problem not in engineering terms but in organic terms. In the engineering mindset, an idea is thought of, the system is instructed and the chain of command is responsible for implementation. This approach does not work when the idea to be implemented involves personal change for the people. They simply don't buy in. They go through the mechanics and then move on.

The better imagery is one of introducing a new gene into a body. The idea is injected and therapy is used to create the conditions under which the body can accept and then gradually learn to adapt. The starting injection is the pilot program.

Once we had convinced top management of the importance of wrapping IBM around markets, we received permission to undertake a small pilot program. We ran into resistance almost at once.

"The problem was that no one wanted to be a pilot." Stephen was faced with a job of persuasion. "We had no shortage of important markets. But all the people we approached were skeptical about the idea. They were all under intense pressure to deliver, and the idea of having to pull together a group to discuss the market seemed like a major amount of work—for a very nebulous reward."

We finally got five groups to agree to work on the problem. But under nontraditional terms. We moved from pilots to prototypes. We were recently with the chairman of one of the Big Six accounting firms, who put the distinction between pilots and prototypes nicely. A pilot is just an idea. No one ever intends or expects it to be implemented. A prototype is more serious—this could be real. We wanted prototypes.

"The early groups were highly successful," Stephen was rapidly gaining confidence that we were on to something. "A remarkable thing happened. People started talking to one another and getting past the years of history that had driven them apart." This turned into a pervasive phenomenon. The fundamental initial problems were ones of ignorance. People had been apart for so long they no longer understood, in sufficient detail, the concerns of each of their colleagues.

"There was a tremendous amount of information sharing. Problems did not miraculously go away, but people began to see the causes at the root of those issues and learn to get at them. By the end of the first six months, none of the prototypes could imagine their community not existing." Stephen had a great story to take to top management. The idea worked and we were to get permission to take on the next wave of twelve more communities.

NETWORKING MADE EASY

"We were part of the second wave of MFCs," says Maurie Prauner, who would become the market opportunity manager charged with bringing the networking MFC together. Networking is the unit within IBM that links together the customer's hardware. It sounds simple, but it is a $5 billion business within IBM. Networking sounds like a product, but in the computer industry people often buy by subject—networking, multimedia, systems management—so it met many of the criteria of a market.

"After our first few sessions, there was no one who had attended the meetings who couldn't see the advantages of the MFC. It was too good to give up," he explains. "It got all the different units of the company talking to one another, and it brought us closer to the customer. Why even think about stopping?"

Why? Because IBM was still set up in the typical pyramid, a pyramid being driven apart by matrix management.

And then, on December 4, 1991, that pyramid crumbled. This was the day that Chairman Akers announced the "quasi-break-up" of the company into its major parts. IBM divided the company into different business units, expected to be profitable and cash supporting on their own. This was the first time the company had presented itself to the world as anything less than a monolith.

The reasoning behind the move was simple: The company was attempting to get its operations on the same economic basis as its niche competitors. To do that, IBM eliminated cross-subsidies, and at the same time freed itself from needless bureaucracy.

"The December announcement introduced a major problem into our MFC, but one we got over because we had already started a tradition of working together. Without that, it would have driven us further apart as we all struggled to make our own operations work," says Prauner. "Of course, it was chaotic at first. No one knew exactly what was going on after the December fourth announcement. But as a result, we were to learn that the molecular form of organization is held together by two things—a shared sense of purpose and market identity, and strongly held shared values. Values, we were to discover, can only hold a group together if their economic interests are addressed first."

"Our MFC is only valuable to its members because it serves their self-interest. It helps them sell more product and it allows them to do their job better. If it didn't, they would not remain part of the group."

The resolution of the long-standing problems in the network world between marketing and development serves as a case in point.

Marketing could see an ever fragmenting market which development could never satisfy, yet development controlled the flow of new product.

Development could see the fragmentation of distribution

channels and new markets opening up. However, marketing controlled market access within a monolithic sales organization increasingly restricted to a narrow segment of the market.

Before the networking MFC, the two divisions were constantly locking horns. When they both became part of the same MFC, they were able to figure out the best way of getting a product to market. Why? Because for the first time, the two divisions actually had an official forum in which to sit down and talk about their shared problems. A forum that was off-line from the traditional decision structure and had rules of cooperative behavior all its own. They sat down and talked to one another about their focus on the customer instead of their internal concerns.

Once they did, marketing discovered the limitations of partnering and outside sourcing. The marketing division had always thought it was a piece of cake for IBM to team up with another vendor, but the people in development were able to explain in detail why that was not the case.

And development learned from marketing just how difficult it is to manage a remote distribution system. A year later, much the wiser, accommodations have been reached or will be reached between the two groups, both working together to establish new markets and distribution channels.

"We are now in the habit of consulting one another," says Prauner. As a direct result, the networking operation is becoming more focused.

"Thanks to the MFC, we discovered that we really didn't know who we were in the marketplace," Prauner says. "This was making it difficult to agree on a whole slew of things, from what we should develop, to what image campaign we wanted, to how we should sell."

But by getting together in a MFC, networking soon realized what the real problem was: They were focusing on the wrong thing. Like all IBM operations of old, it kept looking at technical issues. Should we go after large system users or smaller networks?

Instead, after meeting for a while, the MFC realized that it should be concentrating on the customer. Then having figured out who the customer was, and what he or she needed, they could work backwards and create the product that would satisfy his or her needs.

The new vision statement reflects this new way of thinking:

> IBM's clients bring their worlds together by linking minds and information into knowledge networks.

Their simple but rich vision statement defined what networking was supposed to do. "The positioning discussion was incredibly important," Maurie found, "because our customers were increasingly asking us to link their PCs and microcomputers, and the whole work environment, together. We began to recognize that the mainframe era was over, and that in the future, companies were going to be driven technically by their networks, not their mainframes. By understanding what was going on with our customers, and understanding how we would have to tie all their machines together, we were able to place ourselves in the mainstream."

December fourth almost scuttled this level of understanding. But, it also brought out a reality about market focused communities. They were as important in a break-up scenario as they were in a "single company" scenario. They were addressing the root issue of IBM—how to create integration in its operations, without bureaucracy, so as to yield competitive advantage. In other words, how to mimic the flexibility of its competitors with their access to consortia while accessing the advantage of a single culture. It was this reality that led to the swift acceptance of the idea in IBM.

"By 1993, we had lost count of the number of communities that had been set up. One guess went as high as a thousand. Some were simply people leaping on the bandwagon and renaming existing groups to fall in with what they thought was modern practice, but many were very real. The original groups had spawned subgroups, which spread their influence back into research and forward into the field operations. They were all linked together by a common sense of direction based on the worldwide MFC." Stephen was clear-eyed about the idea. "MFCs worked because they tapped into a real problem. They helped people come together around the market and eliminated contention. They each developed characters appropriate to the markets they were serving and the people who were in them. But none of them would have been successful without initial top management support."

MAKING MFCS WORK

Since doing this pioneering work with IBM, we have introduced the idea of market focused communities in various ways to client situations. One of the most interesting was the Worldwide Fund for Nature under the chairmanship of Prince Philip. Their problem involved bringing together over thirty countries to address the problems of biodiversity on the planet, and, to do it in a way that applied some consistent conservation philosophies, used scarce technical skills most effectively and used up the least amount of precious funds on management. Their solution involved grouping around four major conservation problems, and bringing all the resources of the organization to bear on each of them through what one could call a "problem focused community."

MFCs work in all types of organizations—WWF is a charity. The same principles apply in government, bringing departments together around a social issue. But to make them work you need to follow certain rules.

First, the communities have to be connected to the operational substructure of the business. If they are not linked they float away and become mere talking shops or therapy sessions for disgruntled employees. If that linkage is to happen, the selection of the major communities has to be a decision of the strategic management of the business, and they must be formally blessed as strategic. This clearly happened with WWF when the problem areas were decided upon by the whole organization at its annual general meeting.

Second, taking on the role of running a community must be seen as a route to power. It is a fact that the best executives are ambitious—that's what gives them their edge. If the MFC is seen as an impotent staff role, off-line from the real route to the center of affairs, it will suffer.

Third, the community must take on responsibility for itself, not be the handmaiden of a constituency. This can be seen in the various attempts to set up drug czars and the like in government. Where the person who is in charge is off-line from those who own the resources, there is turf war. The successful community will have communal ownership of the problem. If this seems odd, the alternative has even less success, even when that person has huge budgets with which to entice the cooperation. Like democracy, communal ownership of a common problem is a poor solution. However, all the alternatives are worse!

Finally, while communal ownership is crucial, so is a champion with a real self-interest. Part of the success of the

IBM networking group was due to the fact that Maurie was in the networking operations and had a real personal interest in making the group work. Groups that do not have such a champion are more difficult to form unless they have intense strategic backing from the top of the business. Even then it is tough.

Market focused communities cut across the traditional structure of a pyramidal business, and all its management traditions are addressed, including measurement and personnel appraisal systems. They cannot succeed if a culture of noncooperation is allowed to persist. Putting in the changes in management approach which support them is crucial to their success. Given that, they become the embryo from which a Stage 5 company, completely wrapped around its market, can emerge.

MFCS: PART OF IBM'S FUTURE?

MFCs were introduced into IBM when it was an integrated company in 1990. Yet they survived and thrived when the company embarked on its "break-up" phase in 1991 and 1992. Our bet is that they will be a major gene in the business even as Lou Gerstner reverses the break-up trend and starts to reintegrate the business. The reason is simple—markets are fragmented, moving fast, and crowded with niche competitors and the company needs equally flexible structures throughout itself to respond quickly.

Gerstner's resynthesis of IBM provides the basic framework within which the MFC concept can flourish to an even greater extent. The creation of a strong strategic center with the executive team and its associated strategic groups puts into place a broader spectrum of strategic opinion than existed previously. As this group starts to address the markets where IBM wants to succeed, the MFC gene will, we believe, either come to the fore or be reinvented under a different name. Otherwise, it will be largely unchanged. Our confidence is based on the simple fact that MFCs contain the primary elements for success in such a world—market focus, cross-operational cooperation, dispelling of ignorance and a protected forum where tough issues can be resolved in total openness away from the traditional decision-making structure. Moreover, MFCs are flexible and self-policing, so once they are in place they persist because they solve a problem, not because they are mandated—the only way to go in a world as large and complex as IBM.

Indeed, as we have helped the evolution of several of these groups over the past three years, through the various shifts the company has taken, we have noticed a phenomenon that indicates how far they have settled into the culture. In the early days, one of the major issues was the degree to which continuity was lost in the business as it reorganized. In those three years, tens of thousands of IBMers left the business, with inevitable continuous restructuring of jobs and roles. The MFCs, we have noticed, have provided a source of organizational continuity. A person is no longer a member of a community—his or her role is a member. When the person turns over, the role remains and the new incumbent inherits the seat at the MFC table. But along with that seat is a history of prior decisions—equally inherited. Your colleagues in the community rely on these decisions made in an open forum. It is now difficult to ignore those accumulated agreements, so stability in strategy toward the market results, despite job turnover.

Lou Gerstner sees the challenge—to be centralized and decentralized at the same time and to somehow drive down the middle of the road. We believe MFCs are a key element in that strategy.

STAGE 4 GOLDEN RULES

• **Everyone must have a feel for the market**
The market focused communities brought the customer into the executive suite at IBM. Previously concerned with decision making from studies, executives from different parts of the business now wrestle directly with customer issues as a team. This creates much more informed decisions while speeding up the company's responses, since market and product issues are addressed simultaneously instead of by separate functions at different times. For the first time, the true fragmentation of the market has started to become clear, and in networking, for example, immense strides were made in obtaining a detailed understanding of customer needs.

• **Reinvent the management system**
Breaking down barriers between parts of the company was a major issue. In common with most large complex companies, IBM had many walls between its people, walls stiffened by an aggressively individual measurement system. The communities strengthened people's understanding of the business issues facing each other, and that understanding brought down the walls. Once people had experienced cooperation, they could not walk away from it. However, that in itself would not have been enough without top-level sponsorship in the early months. Even then, the traditional system was resistant and some groups deteriorated into "talking shops" or "therapy sessions" where people went to commiserate with

one another. When this happened, the groups slowly died as people ceased to attend under the pressure of time or managers sent lower-level staff.

• Top management cooperation isn't a given

In companies with a strong individual tradition and powerful, ambitious personalities—the people who make things happen—cooperation has to be built in. IBM now has a tradition of top executive cooperation in serving the customer. Today MFCs are recognized as a valid form of organizational response to the customer. If they did not exist, they would have to be invented. As the management structure is pared down, MFCs will become more and more important for driving the company's response to the customer.

Aetna: Improve
or Die

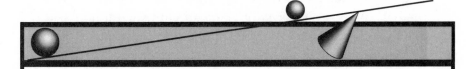

The peculiar thing about the life insurance industry is
that it is probably the most risk averse, and therefore
one of the most resistant to change. The roles and
organizational structure are highly traditional; anything new is seen as a threat.

The life insurance industry thinks in terms of decades or even centuries, rather than business quarters
or years. This perspective, combined with the risk-
averse culture, leads to the snail's-pace rate of change.

However, incredible things can happen when an
organization has its back to the wall. Working with
Aetna's Individual Life business, we saw them leap
straight to Stage 5 and learned that a company can

achieve dramatic cost savings by creating a truly entrepreneurial culture and supporting organization. The key was to create incentives to build the business and self-regulate costs. The results of Aetna's efforts were to turn the industry on its head.

Looking at him now, beaming in his oak-paneled office in Hartford, Connecticut, it's hard to imagine that things had not always been this good for Mike Stephen. But it wasn't all that long ago the sixty-year-old president of Aetna International didn't have it so good. In fact, just a few years before, there had been serious talk of eliminating the division he had been running, Aetna of Canada, and (by implication) his job.

The problem Mike faced back then was as simple as it is common. Aetna of Canada was a medium-sized fish in a very crowded pond. Of the 170 companies selling life insurance in Canada, Aetna ranked about tenth. Margins had been cut in an attempt to grow market share, but in a flat market, all that does is touch off a price war, leaving Aetna worse off than before. It was still a small fish, but now it was a small fish that wasn't very profitable.

The solution, as the people back at corporate headquarters in Hartford saw it, was simple, albeit brutal. Sell the company. Take whatever we can get. If we can't find a buyer, then we should just shut it down. Yes, the move would have the potential to throw as many as a thousand people out of work, but better that than barely breaking even every year. The division continued to tie up huge amounts of capital, and there was just no way that it was ever going to hit its goal of 15 percent return on investment. If the division was sold—or shuttered—all that money could, in the eyes of corporate, be put to better use.

Not surprisingly, the news didn't go over well in the Canadian division, which asked for more time to turn things around. That wasn't something the folks at headquarters wanted to grant. But you can't be seen as someone who shuts down entire divisions arbitrarily. Headquarters agreed to hire a consulting firm to come and take a look.

In theory, the high-priced New York–based consultants would come in, sketch a few organizational matrixes that should be followed to return the division to profitability, and everyone would live happily ever after. The reality was nobody was expecting much. The consultants were expected to rubber-stamp a decision that had already been made. It was just a matter of time until the division would be shut down.

Learning of headquarters' plan, Mike Stephen rebelled. Thirty years in the industry had left Stephen with the deep-seated belief that the problem at Aetna wasn't volume, but the way that the company did business. He couldn't prove it. He couldn't buttress his case by generating a series of matrixes or by pointing to the result of a regression analysis as the consultants would when recommending shutting down his division. Still, he knew he was right.

Part of his conviction stemmed from the people he had hired. He turned to two of them—Bill Fearn and Pat Beaudoin—to help develop a plan that would turn the division around, knowing full well that the clock was ticking. The consultants headquarters was sending would arrive in Mike's office in less than a month.

Standing next to Mike, Bill could not have looked more different. Where Mike had the lean build of a man who ran three miles every day before lunch, Bill, in his mid-forties, was heavyset with the powerful build of a former hockey player. And whereas Mike was a salesman—he began his business career as an insurance agent—Bill was the numbers guy. The numbers, Bill was convinced, showed fat everywhere within the company. His job was to provide Mike with the tools to clean up the firm. And he was going to do it. He wasn't going to have a failure on his résumé. As a former assistant deputy minister in the Canadian government and an accountant, Bill was used to success—cutting costs was one way to achieve it—and this current assignment would be no different. In practice, Bill's role turned out to be crucial. As we looked at options, he worked with the actuaries to build a financial model of the business that gave immense credibility to the proposed solutions.

If the company was going to turn around, Pat, who headed human resources, would have a huge part to play. Tall and elegant, she had already set about solving one huge problem at the company: turnover.

"We had 40 percent turnover in the clerical staff every year. Some of that was the overheated local economy. But the retraining costs [every time a replacement worker was hired he or she would have to be trained] and lost productivity caused by waiting for that replacement employee to start work were simply burying the company," she recalled. "We'd start the trend downward by working on the work conditions and job specs. These jobs were outright boring. Obviously, we had to change that and make the jobs more attractive and interesting."

While this obviously was important, it paled in comparison to the task of justifying the division's existence to headquarters. Unless that could be done, there would be no clerical workers to worry about because there would be no clerical work for them to do. Aetna would be out of business.

There would be a fourth major player in the drama: Nick Villani, the sales manager. Nick had been one of the best salesmen in Aetna of Canada's history, taking a major pay cut to come into the head office to work with Mike, Bill and Pat as vice president in charge of sales. Everyone knew that his promotion meant he was taking home less money. Nick felt that when you're giving customers a discount, you always tell them. It's a basic rule of selling.

Big and jovial, Nick had just had triple bypass surgery. Released in record time, he was held in awe by his doctors, who were amazed by the speed of his recovery. But while they were surprised, Nick clearly was not. Just another example of positive thinking, he would say.

In a business where an agent gets rejected dozens of times a day, Nick's ability to motivate people and keep them up emotionally was legendary. The sales force worshiped Nick. Whatever he had to say about Mike's plan to save the division would be a critical factor in both its success and its holding the business together during a time of massive change.

And massive change was imperative, or Aetna of Canada would die.

THE CRISIS

When we first met Mike and his team, the consultants that the home office had hired were on their way—or would have been if Mike hadn't kept stalling them. His delaying tactics bought us a month, and that was enough for us to get under way. We were well into our first workshop when the executives back at headquarters found out what Mike was up to.

"Get those consultants out of there," they said, not thrilled. "Fast! You aren't going to make the decisions about the future of the division, we are. Now get them out of there. Now!"

Mike's response was a bit more polite, but just as clear:

"Not if you want a business that's worth anything when it comes time for you to sell it, I won't. You've got to give us a shot of doing it our way."

Mike patiently explained his reasoning. Once it became known that Aetna was bringing in high-priced consultants to evaluate what was going on in Canada, everybody in the industry would start assuming that the division was for sale. Not only would that instantly reduce the potential price the division could fetch—after all, who will pay top dollar knowing the seller is willing to part with the merchandise at just about any price?—but the insurance brokers who handled Aetna's lines would start bailing out. No broker wants to sell policies of a company that may not be around next week. If that happens, sales will collapse and the value of the division will have fallen dramatically long before the consultants hired by headquarters could prepare their first flow chart.

Mike's argument was strong enough for headquarters to reconsider. They were willing to back down—temporarily.

"Maybe," the response eventually came back, "we should meet these guys you want to hire, Mike."

We flew down to Hartford in late May and convinced the senior staff that they didn't have a whole lot to lose by giving us a shot. They agreed, if for no other reason than to make sure that they had covered every possible base for determining the division's fate. We were giving a stay of execution, albeit a short one. We had until Labor Day to deliver a report to explain how Aetna of Canada could be saved.

With that, we set out to reinvent the process of selling life insurance.

We began with the fundamental question: Who is the customer? There were only two choices—the consumer and the agent. At first the consumer won—after all, he was the person who paid for the product—but the problem with focusing on the consumer became obvious within seconds. There just was no way to create a competitive advantage.

The problem was knock-off time. It could take up to three years to develop a new life insurance product, put all the back office systems in place to support it and gain the regulatory approval needed to sell it. Unfortunately, once you got that approval, competitors could knock you off in no time flat. They could have the identical, or at least substantially similar, product on the market in a matter of weeks.

Could you gain an advantage with consumers through your sales force? Maybe someone could, but not Aetna. Everyone uses the same independent brokers, who pick and choose the products they want to sell from a wide variety of companies. The only way to get a competitive advantage through the salesman was through the captive agents—i.e., Aetna's salespeople. And while Aetna's salespeople were good, they were not significantly better than the other brokers, and there were not enough of them to gain any kind of economies of scale.

That left the broker/agent as the customer, and the problems there seem to be identical to focusing on either the independents or the captive sales force.

We were pondering all this when Nick rose to the occasion. "What we need," he said somewhat wistfully, "is a franchise."

And with that, one of the most original ideas to hit the life insurance industry was born.

DID YOU HEAR THE ONE ABOUT THE INSURANCE AGENT AND . . .

A little bit about the selling of insurance. Typically, there are two types of salespeople. Independent brokers, who have their own businesses and receive commissions on the products they sell, and agents, who are employees of the insurance company.

The brokers receive good commissions, but from the insurance company's point of view, they are a variable cost. They get paid only if they sell. That's the good news; the bad news is that they are not loyal. They sell a variety of products from a variety of insurance companies. They pick the offerings they want from an insurance company's line—selling whatever policy pays them most and best serves their customers—and ignore the rest of the line. This results in very competitive pricing and the products becoming commodity-like.

Agents are loyal. They must sell only what the insurance company employing them has to offer, but they are expensive. They traditionally receive a salary during the first couple of years they work for the company, in addition to commission. And even agents of long standing are given an income guarantee. Worse, the best ones promptly leave and become brokers, frequently competing with the insurance company that trained them.

The business wasn't wonderful, but as long as financial service companies were regulated—with all the players battling to keep their prices in line—there wasn't a whole lot of risk. All the companies would win or lose together.

But deregulation throughout the 1980s changed all that. Price wars became rampant, as new players, most notably Canada's large banks, tried to enter the industry. Insurance companies such as Aetna—with neither overwhelming size nor a specialized niche—found themselves steadily losing ground, and money. When the industry was regulated, insurance companies could pay policyholders less than market rates on whole life policies—those which offered a savings component. Once the industry was deregulated, insurance companies had to pay competitive rates. That, of course, put tremendous pressure on margins.

How could you compete in this new environment? Suddenly a traditional agency sales force didn't look that great. Those salespeople came complete with high fixed costs. Becoming totally dependent on brokers didn't have much appeal either. That would give them too much power to decide your fate.

What was needed, as Nick hit on intuitively, was some sort of hybrid, and creating franchisees would fill the bill. With a franchise system you would offload your expenses on a dedicated sales force. Why would the sales force go along? They stood to make more money, since they would be able to pick and choose the products they offered, and shifting the cost burden didn't have to be onerous. The sales force would have direct control over costs and could eliminate anything it thought to be superfluous.

The idea was sound. Aetna would take its existing sales force and make them franchisees. They would run their own business inside a common framework and under a common name. It would be the best of both worlds.

To make the idea work, the company would have to change not only the relationship with its sales force but the way it did business. Under the new arrangement, it would have to source product from throughout the industry. If Aetna could create what the people out in the field wanted, great. If not, they would get it from someone else. Under the new arrangement, Aetna would offer the agents and brokers a full product line that was guaranteed to be content and price competitive. Aetna would also provide administrative help.

The last was key. What insurance salespeople, whether brokers or agents, value most is sales time in front of a customer. Time, or money spent administering the business—

filling out forms and reconciling commission statements—costs them money two different ways. Not only is there a cost to pay someone to file or process the information, but supervising that function keeps the salesperson from selling.

As it was, the salespeople had too many administrative problems. A broker selling, say, five differing companies' products would receive five different statements, all unique and all needing to be double-checked.

Inherent from the beginning of Aetna's plan was providing administrative tools and procedures that would make the agent's life easier.

HOW DO YOU PULL THIS OFF?

While the idea of creating franchisees made intuitive sense to Mike, Pat, Nick and Bill, we knew it would be greeted with total incomprehension elsewhere. The agents would be skeptical. Why was the company doing it? How would it affect their commissions? Why should they want to be entrepreneurs? They liked their relationship with Aetna just as it was.

The branch managers, who supervised the agents, would hate it. It was obviously a loss of status for them—and increased risk. How did they control agents who owned their own business? They would go from being managers to support staff the moment the franchising program went into effect.

The internal staff wouldn't be crazy about it. Some functions, most notably information processing, would be shifted out to the field, and obviously, the more things were decentralized, the less need there would be to have a corporate staff.

It would be a difficult program to sell, and it would be

flat out impossible if the parent company was not on board. The whole thing would boil down to a presentation in September. Mike and his staff would have to convince their bosses that the franchise idea was the way to go—the only way to go.

We lost count of the number of what-ifs that were run, but no matter how many times we ran the numbers, we kept getting the same answer: Creating franchisees was the way to go. The biggest benefit of the plan was that all the marketing costs would be shifted to the franchisee. That made sense because the franchisee was the best person to control them. He would know what he needed to do his job and what he didn't.

What would be Aetna's role once the new plan was in place? The company would serve, in essence, as a manufacturer, supplying the franchisee with product to sell. The easiest analogy to the system we would be trying to create is the relationship that exists between car companies and their dealers.

"We had a major story to tell," Mike recalls. "This was a complete reinvention of the insurance business. The presentation to the people in Hartford went well, very well. We received another stay of execution. We were given four months to work on the idea and see if we could make it real. While they were intrigued by what we wanted to accomplish, they wanted to know whether it was actually doable."

It was time to sell the program.

Getting the agents on board was crucial. If they were not behind the plan, they would end up leaving to sell insurance for someone else, no matter how wonderful the franchisee plan looked on paper. The problem was how to convince them that becoming franchisees was a good thing.

The easiest way to do this was to have the agents help create the franchisee program. It's hard to hate something you helped build. But with about 150 agents out in the field, it was impossible to get them all involved. Still, input from the agents was critical. What to do?

The solution was simple. Pick a small group of agents and managers, swear them to secrecy, compensate them for time away from the field, have them come in to learn about the franchisee plan and give Mike, Bill, Pat and Nick their reaction.

Bill Myles was the company's top agent. A multi-million-dollar seller, he was knowledgeable about a whole range of personal insurance products, but he was worried once he heard the plan.

"The problem, as I saw it, was that I was going to be deluged with administration once I became a franchisee," he recalled. "I know they said that wouldn't happen, but I thought it was a real possibility."

Bill was also concerned about the product the company was going to offer. Could Aetna deliver on its promise to deliver a broad range of product?

He made it painfully clear what was at stake. "If the company did not deliver, I would transfer my loyalty to another company. I'm a good salesman. The relationship with the policyholder was mine. He would go with me if I switched to someone else."

Jack Major was the manager based in Calgary. His view was slightly different. Switching to a franchisee system would mean a great loss of status, as far as he was concerned.

In his present job, he had a corner office in a prestigious office building in the core of downtown. Once a franchisee system went into effect, his office would be in the back of his car, going from franchisee to franchisee to determine how he could make their lives better.

"In Bill's case it was simple. He had his customers," Jack told us. "All I had was the ability to organize, train and motivate people. If I was not careful, I would find myself in the same position, on a smaller scale, that the company was in. I would train people and they would either leave me or pass me by. After years of being in charge, by nature of my rank and title, I would have to decide what my value added was. That was a very humbling thing to do."

Armed with the concerns of employees, we set out to sell the program. The task of selling the salespeople, Mike Stephen knew, could only go to Nick, the ultimate salesperson.

"The agents trusted him," Stephen explains. "They would believe him and take his lead. He was their man. They would not have taken it from me, even though I was an old agent, and knew most of them personally. We needed Nick to hold them together. They had all kinds of personal worries, worries about income, retirement, company commitment. Nick would have to be the one to address them. And he did, one at a time, and in small groups throughout the country. He explained, in detail, what the franchisee program was all about and stressed over and over again how the salesmen could make more money on the arrangement."

"But in the end," Stephen explains, "it all boiled down to trust."

"The salesmen trusted Nick, and so they decided to go along."

THE INTERNAL STAFF

The big losers in all this were, of course, members of the internal staff. They were the costs that the company hoped to save. Getting them to buy into the program was each department manager's responsibility. The managers could— and indeed often did—turn to Pat for help.

"The key to making this work internally was buy-in," Pat explained. "But you can't get buy-in without allowing the people to understand what was expected of them, and allowing them the opportunity to change their work patterns."

In other words, Aetna gave people the chance to reinvent their jobs. And the job they were inventing would be far different.

It is natural in a big company to see your job in terms of function: "I am a marketing person"; "I do internal auditing"; "I handle accounts receivable." Descriptions like this are the inevitable result of applying Henry Ford's image of the assembly line to the rest of the workplace.

The problem with this approach is it separates the worker back at headquarters from the people out in the field actually generating the sale. Insurance agents selling whole life policies don't particularly know, or care, what somebody in internal auditing does. All they know is that policies were sold, and part of the money they think they should rightfully receive is being withheld for something called overhead.

The new system would make that "overhead"—i.e., the people back at corporate headquarters—directly responsible to the people doing the selling. If they could justify the amount of money they were costing the franchisees, they would continue to have a job. If they couldn't, then the franchisee would buy the service elsewhere.

Information systems serve as a case in point.

It turns out Aetna was making the change over to franchisees at a critical point in Information Systems history. The company was about to make a multi-million-dollar expansion to its mainframe—a lot of it justified by the needs of the life sales operation. We suggested they didn't. For one thing, given the pressure being applied by corporate, this was the wrong moment to be spending millions. For another, it became clear to us that once the changeover was complete, they wouldn't need a mainframe at all. The centralization and control of information is fine when you are running a large bureaucratic organization, but that wouldn't be the new Aetna. The new Aetna would be a series of small, independent offices linked to a relatively small central staff.

If you are building a flexible system that can adapt to local circumstances, you must put the maximum amount of intelligence and function at the lowest point of the system— in this case, on the desks of the franchisees. Only issues that require system-wide coordination should be kicked up to a higher level. The problem of having a mainframe was not the cost of the machine (they were working on secondhand equipment that was not expensive) as much as it was the mainframe mentality. Everything has to be centralized, and the loss of flexibility in the business as a whole that comes from having a slow computing environment makes it difficult to adapt quickly and get product to the market fast.

To his credit, the IS manager was an open-minded person, and he embraced the inevitable, which involved him turning his position on information processing 180 degrees. IS went from having a mainframe bias to having a dispersed intelligence bias. As a result, Aetna reinvented its entire approach to IS and put true intelligence on the agent's desk, or wherever he or she needs it. The result was the creation of a highly flexible system that put Aetna two or three years ahead of its competitors, who were still dominated by the mainframe mentality.

CHANGES IN ATTITUDES

Changing the way the company operated was relatively easy. Changing the way people thought about their jobs was harder.

Part of the shift occurred naturally. As more and more responsibility was pushed out into the field, the number of people needed back at headquarters steadily decreased. The internal staff shrank by more than 25 percent once the shift to creating franchisees was completely in place.

And as it shrank, the company—to the surprise of some —began to work better.

"We started to see each other as people again, not functions," says one middle-level manager. "Communications improved. There was a greater sense of cohesion and purpose, and things happened much faster."

Speed was something neither Aetna nor any other insurance company was noted for. According to Mike Stephen, this stems in part from the nature of the product the industry sells.

"Insurance is different," he says. "We have policies in place dating back to 1898. We spend our lives dealing with risks that are spread out over decades, over whole human lifetimes. Slow variables are our lifeblood. Unlike most industries, our problem is not thinking long-term, but short-term. And when we think short-term, we have a simple and counterintuitive way of boosting profits. Stop selling. If you stop selling, you stop paying commissions, but you still get to collect premiums from the policies you have previously sold. If you take this route, profitability soars."

Given the way the industry thinks, it is not surprising that everything seemed to move at glacial speed. Products were produced slowly. Claims were paid eventually. Names of policyholders registered in the system someday.

That's just the way it was.

But over the three years of shifting the business over to franchisees, the company had materially sped up its thinking.

Once committed to delivering the best possible product to the franchisees, regardless of whether they actually prepared that product themselves, Aetna began moving much faster. They had no choice. The market demanded it.

And the agents demanded it. In the past, the staff back at headquarters had no real incentive to satisfy the agent. Oh, sure, everyone said that the agent was important, but if an agent wasn't taken care of when he asked for something, nothing bad happened. The people at corporate still had their jobs, and if the agent was unhappy that he didn't get the document he needed, or his check was ten days late, well, where was he going to go?

"To another company," now came the response, once the franchise system was in place.

When your job back at headquarters is to make the agent happy, and you may very well find yourself out of work if you don't, all of a sudden you begin to pay attention to your customer's needs.

THE END RESULT

Aetna Life survived, prospered and changed the way the industry viewed the sale of insurance. For a long time after the transition to a franchisee-driven operation was complete, the model Mike Stephen helped create was something that everyone in the industry—including, ironically, the people back at the home office in Hartford—wanted to learn about. Mike was a hero, and based on the transformation at Aetna Canada he was named to head all of international operations.

It is easy, when you look at what he accomplished in Canada, to understand why. Costs were cut over 25 percent, and more important, they truly became controllable for the first time as a result of being shifted to the field. Now the people who had a direct interest in how much money was being spent, the franchisees, could determine what was truly needed. A clerk back at headquarters probably didn't care what the company was spending for rubber bands, health care or computers. His or her paycheck wasn't directly affected one way or the other. But the franchisees care passionately. Every dollar comes out of their potential profits.

No wonder costs went down after the franchisee program was in place, and the company's return on investment began to rise substantially. The company was finally heading to profitability.

The changes Mike instigated are still working their way out. The new life insurance operations are at Stage 5—flexible, fast moving, with new economics, a new culture and a new way of making decisions. With this prototype understood, Aetna Canada is transforming all of its operations with expectations of returns as dramatic as the initial work.

STAGE 5 GOLDEN RULES

- **You've got to hug the customer**
Aetna defined the agent as its primary focus, the place where it could get competitive advantage by having the best agents in the business. It created the "Agents' Insurance Company," putting in systems and approaches which completely wrapped the whole business around each franchise individually. This pinpoint focus in the market was confirmed when Aetna made its first major expansion of the franchise force. The level of take-up by those approached was almost 100 percent.

- **Phew! We made it!**
Aetna achieved the practically impossible, making a flying leap to fully molecular. To do this Mike needed the tenacity of a bulldog—driving the concept forward. Once that the system was in place, the challenge was to exploit its flexibility. This is more difficult than it sounds. The effort

required to get to Stage 5 in one shot can so exhaust the players that they can't raise the energy to exploit their good fortune. If they can, the potential is enormous as customers are attracted to the system by its very flexibility in serving their needs.

• **No pain, no control**

The use of self-regulation in costs is incredibly powerful as a means of ensuring that overhead structures remain low in cost and highly flexible. The risk, however, is that self-management of costs becomes "selfish" management for personal gain. To avoid that, a complementary set of strong values around cooperation for the common good has to be established. Involving the franchisees in management and discipline of the system becomes important, giving them a sense of being part of a whole and ensuring quality control over the way the common asset—the name and positioning of the company—is used.

All Paths Lead to the Summit

We have just seen half a dozen organizations in the midst of a major transition. They come from very different industries, with very different cultures and competitive environments.

Each approached change from their own particular starting point: building cross functional teams, becoming market driven, introducing total quality management and so forth. However, like a mountain being scaled by many climbers, they are ultimately on a journey to the same summit.

In these journeys, we served as guides, moving the people into higher and higher levels of understanding. As the climbers ascended, they crossed key boundaries: the end of the tree line, the snow line and finally the sunlit uplands.

Not all members of the team climbed at the same rate of

speed. Some sprinted ahead, then fell behind. Some plodded steadily, rationing their energy for the long haul. Others simply tired easily and dropped out. Still, the stages of the climb, from base camp to summit, became clear.

Everyone had to decide to take the climb and get away from Stage 1. They all needed to get strong top management cooperation and an agreement that the old world could no longer solve their problems. As they moved to Stage 2 they put teamwork and cooperation in place. People learned how to work in teams and gained a broader alignment around a common strategy and destination. In Stage 3, they started to explore the implications of mass customization technology. Teamwork became cross-operational as they sought to mold themselves to a range of customers in different segments. In Stage 4, they faced up to the managerial assumptions that were preventing true customer focus. By installing such ideas as market focused communities, they started to break up the monolithic management approaches of the past. By Stage 5, they had created the conditions under which they could use their ability to create variety at low cost as a strategic weapon. These stages have become familiar to us in many different situations and recognizing their existence is almost a critical success factor needed for making the transition.

However, no journey can be taken without leadership at all places in the organization. This change cannot be mandated. Nor is it restricted to those at the top. You are part of it regardless of where your position in the organization or what nominal title you hold. Everyone is a part of this change. If we are all in this together, what are the keys to making the shift happen?

• **Create a flag.** It is always easier to rally around a common enemy than to get warring factions to agree on anything on their own. If you were to lock New Age Democrats, Dixie Democrats, traditional Democrats and the other various Democratic factions in a room, the odds are they would never agree on much of anything.

However, remind them an election is coming up, and they'll all unite instantly to defeat their Republican opponent. During the Persian Gulf War you had people from France, England, America—countries that don't always see eye to eye—working side by side. They were united behind a common goal: getting Saddam Hussein. Even though these people had little in common, they worked so well together that the land war was over in a hundred hours.

In creating a flag you must look outside your organization. Focus on your customer. If you are business, your flag is your customer; insist that everything you do be designed to make the customer's life better. Focus around a social issue if you are in government.

If you start wrapping every function of your organization around your customer, it is easy for the warring factions in places such as marketing, research and development, and information processing to work together. The key is making sure that whatever flag you decide upon is outside your company. If it is too close to one group, others might not go along.

• **Start small.** We would like to say that the story about the CEO who got religion on quality from a book he bought in an airport bookstore was made up. It isn't. It's true. But we've seen worse. There was a chairman who decided his company need a corporate culture. He summoned his top managers and told them to create one—by next Friday.

There is a natural tendency, in trying to change a corporation, for the chairman to stand up in front of a group and order things to change. But ordering up an instant corporate culture—or any other kind of significant corporate change—just doesn't work. Organizations are filled with people, and it is hard to get a huge number of people to agree on anything. And it's even harder to get them to alter their behavior. Oh, sure, they will go through the motions and provide lip service to whatever new idea the chairman has. (After all, nobody wants to be fired for insubordination.) But things won't really change.

People become comfortable with the way they have always done things, and they won't do them differently unless they see a compelling reason to change. Eventually the chairman's new, sweeping idea will die from inertia.

The easiest way to change an organization is to start small. Work on changing one team or one department, and then move on to a second and a third. Just like a snowball rolling downhill, you will achieve critical mass and create an avalanche. But, if you try to move that snow with a hundred bulldozers, they will just get in each other's way and slow everything.

• **Treat resistance as a friend.** There will be tremendous resistance to change. Instead of being frustrated by that fact, a manager should try to use the resistance to his advantage, just as fighters employing judo use the opponent's strength to their advantage.

You must recognize that resistance is a natural part of the change process. Think of the resistance as being like the antibodies that a body produces to fight off a heart transplant. The new heart may be needed, but the body's natural defenses will still spring into effect to reject anything new, including that much needed heart.

Remember when this is all over, everyone has to have reinvented their job. Getting people involved in that process is the best way of dispelling resistance. The natural tendency is to order the people at the bottom of the organization, who actually do the work, to change in a certain way. That's wrong. They probably know exactly what has to change. All you have to do is ask them.

• **Provide a sense of destination.** A vision is not

enough. People want to know where the organization will be once the journey is done. They also want to know, "What's in it for me?"

The changes managers will be asking their people to make are wrenching. They are being uprooted and repeatedly replanted. People want to know that there is an end point, a structure toward which all this is evolving.

The Molecular Organization plays this role. When people who have gone through this process see the new image, they identify with it and are calmed by it. It has a logic and a sense that they can work with. It brings closure when they suspect that the old images they are working with are worn out.

• **Change by design.** Organizations can change by chance. But it is better to change them by design.

The creation and evolution of the change process is a central leadership role. In managing change, the leader must allow for the avalanche effect. He must manage the resistance and monitor the rate at which change is taking place.

Just kicking an idea off is the easy part of a change. A leader who will not see the change process all the way through will not win.

THE MOLECULAR ORGANIZATION: THE MOST NATURAL IN THE WORLD

As you've seen, the Molecular Organization is a natural one. It is the way people organize on their own if there is no formal structure. And while each of the companies profiled took a different route to the summit, they shared certain natural characteristics: They became wrapped around the customer, created flat, empowered organizations, put in place self-regulating cost structures and created customized products and services.

Perhaps most important is that the perilous journeys we described were undertaken by regular folk, not mountain climbers. They all succeeded through grit and determination, combined with a clear vision of the summit: a natural form of organization shaped like a molecule.

Each of you is probably somewhere on the same journey. Fortunately for you, the paths are already in place, the routes marked and the destination known.

All you have to do is let the customer take you there.

Bibliography

Those of us pioneering organizational change in these times of revolutionary transformation rarely find the insights we need from the standard management texts. Our stimulus tends to come from readings outside the corpus of business books. This bibliography is a reflection of some of our readings. The following books have stimulated us and provided us with ideas, metaphors and models.

Abernathy, William J. *The Productivity Dilemma. Roadblock to Innovation in the Automobile Industry.* Baltimore: Johns Hopkins University Press, 1978.

Arendt, Hannah. *On Revolution.* London: Penguin Books, 1965.

Ashby, W. Ross. *An Introduction to Cybernetics.* New York: John Wiley & Sons, 1963.

Bardwick, Judith M. *Danger in the Comfort Zone.* New York: Amacom, 1991.

Beer, Stafford. *Brain of the Firm.* New York: John Wiley & Sons, 1975.

———. *The Heart of Enterprise.* New York: John Wiley & Sons, 1979.

———. *Platform for Change.* New York: John Wiley & Sons, 1975.

von Bertalanffy, Ludwig. *General Systems Theory*. New York: George Braziller, 1968.

Brinton, Crane. *The Anatomy of Revolution*. New York: Vintage Books, 1965.

Burke, Edmund. *Reflections on the Revolution in France*. London: Penguin Books.

Capra, Fritjof. *The Turning Point*. New York: Bantam, 1982.

Davis, Stanley M. *Future Perfect*. New York: Addison-Wesley, 1987.

Dennison, Daniel R. *Corporate Culture and Organizational Effectiveness*. New York: John Wiley & Sons, 1990.

Gleick, James. *Chaos. Making a New Science*. New York: Viking, 1987.

Handy, Charles. *The Age of Unreason*. Boston: Harvard Business School Press, 1989.

Hobsbawm, Eric, and Ranger, Terence, eds. *The Invention of Tradition*. Cambridge: Cambridge University Press, 1983.

Jantsch, Erich. *The Self-Organizing Universe*. New York: Pergamon, 1980.

Jay, Anthony. *Management and Machiavelli*. New York: Penguin Books, 1967.

Kanter, Rosabeth, et al. *The Challenge of Organizational Change*. New York: Free Press, 1992.

Kantrow, Alan M. *The Constraints of Corporate Tradition*. New York: Harper & Row, 1984.

Keen, Peter. *Shaping the Future*. Cambridge: Harvard Business School Press, 1991.

Kennedy, Paul. *The Rise and Fall of the Great Powers*. New York: Random House, 1987.

Levy, Stephen. *Artificial Life. The Quest for a New Creation*. New York: Pantheon, 1992.

Lorenz, Konrad. *On Aggression*. New York: Harcourt Brace, 1974.

Mackay, Charles. *Extraordinary Popular Delusions and the Madness of Crowds*. New York: Harmony Books, 1980.

Mills, D. Quinn. *Rebirth of the Corporation*. New York: John Wiley & Sons, 1993.

Mintzberg, Henry. *Mintzberg on Management. Inside Our Strange World of Organizations*. New York: Free Press, 1989.

Morgan, Gareth. *Images of Organization*. Beverly Hills: Sage, 1986.

Nisbet, Robert. *The Social Philosophers. Community and Conflict in Western Thought,* concise and updated. New York: Washington Square Press, 1982.

Peppoers, Don, and Rogers, Martha. *The One-to-One Future*. New York: Currency Doubleday, 1993.

Schama, Simon. *Citizens. A Chronicle of the French Revolution*. New York: Knopf, 1989.

Smith, Adam. *The Wealth of Nations*. New York: Penguin Books, 1986.

Thompson, James D. *Organizations in Action*. New York: McGraw-Hill, 1967.

Tichy, Noel. *Managing Strategic Change*. New York: John Wiley & Sons, 1983.

Womack, James P., Jones, Daniel T., and Roos, Daniel. *The Machine That Changed the World*. New York: Maxwell Macmillan International, 1990.

Wood, Gordon S. *The Radicalism of the American Revolution*. New York: Knopf, 1992.

Zuboff, Shoshana. *The Age of the Smart Machine*. New York: Basic Books, 1988.

Index

Abernathy, William, 26
accountability, 33, 100, 130, 170
Aetna of Canada, 6, 44, 189–207
  computer system of, 202–3
  costs cut at, 205–6, 207
  employee turnover in, 192
  franchising of, 195, 197, 198–207
  job reinvention in, 202
  planned sale of, 190, 194
  slowness of, 204
airlines, 38, 39, 92–93
Akers, John, 163, 169, 180
allometric growth, 167
amoebas, 17–18
Anheuser-Busch, 29
"antibodies," skepticism and resistance as, 85–86, 88, 212
Apple, 166
asset utilization, 8
atoms, 15, 16–17, 19
Ault Foods, 6, 43, 135–57
  in "commodity trap," 140, 141–45
  customers and, 147–50
  employee empowerment in, 144–45, 146

mass customization in, 151–53, 154, 155, 156
new executive team in, 136–37, 138, 139
yogurt made by, 137, 141, 148, 150–53, 154
automobile industry, 22, 23–24, 26–27, 38, 42

banks, 41, 42
Beaudoin, Pat, 191, 192, 193, 198, 200, 201–2
beer, 29
behavioral change, 7, 115, 118, 120, 212
Ben & Jerry's, 39, 148
bicycles, 155
bosses, 20
  commitment to change needed by, 87, 112–13
  functions of, 15–17
  in Molecular Organization, 15–16, 17
  in pyramid structure, 15, 16
  see also leadership; management
Buick, 26
business perspective, lack of, 134

MICHAEL J. KAY is managing partner of Change Lab International and has over twenty years of experience as a consultant and executive helping organizations change. He has worked with companies in many industries. Mr. Kay has an MA from Cambridge University and an MBA from the London Business School, England.

Dr. GERALD H. B. ROSS is a co-founder and senior partner of Change Lab International. Named one of the top new management gurus by *Business Week*, he is a world-renowned expert on change management. Ross works closely with Vice President Al Gore in the Clinton administration's efforts to reinvent government. He is the creator of *Power of Change*, a best-selling videotape series on corporate transformation.